The

Phenomenon of Obedience

The
Phenomenon of Obedience

Michael Esses

Logos International
Plainfield, New Jersey

to Dr. Ralph Wilkerson
who has shown me the love of Christ
and the phenomenon of obedience in his Life.

Editor's Note

The text of this book has been prepared from tapes of Michael Esses' live teaching sessions at Melodyland Christian Center in Anaheim, California, in early 1973. Because quotations from various standard versions of the Holy Bible were so interwoven with Esses' inimitable paraphrases and amplification, it was deemed appropriate to preserve them that way in the printed text, without the encumbrance of scholarly separation and specific citations. General Scripture references are given at the head of each chapter, however, to guide the reader wishing to consult specific references in his own Bible.

It is our prayer that the result has been the preservation of a more than usual liveliness in these Bible studies, and that God will be glorified as the Holy Spirit quickens His Word throughout these pages.

Contents

Preface

"Obedience, obedience, obedience—this word goes over and over in my mind like a broken record. The many times of disobedience and the few times of obedience in my life."

The lines are quoted from *Michael, Michael, Why Do You Hate Me?* They embody the thought that set me searching out the lives of some of the great men of the Bible.

As I looked at these lives, with the concepts of obedience and disobedience in my mind, I began to see a pattern emerge. It soon became clear that as the day follows the night, God's blessing follows obedience, and His chastisement follows disobedience. It wasn't long before *The Phenomenon of Obedience* began to take shape.

We would all like to think we can be children to a heavenly Father who will be lenient with us, who will close at least one eye and let us get away with our mischief. A Father who will never exact the price for our sins, and who will lovingly indulge us as we commit our acts of disobedience.

If any of you subscribe to this, my advice to you is to forget it.

Our heavenly Father emerges from the pages of the Bible as a loving, kind, and wonderfully patient Father, but He does reward the good and punishes the bad.

Whether you are a petulant Jonah sitting with a gourd over your head, or a repentant David on your knees asking for forgiveness, God requires you to be obedient.

The biblical world was shaped by the obedience and disobedience of its people, and so is our world today.

The nature of man seems to hold out its arms to the concept that we can dance without paying the piper, but God's law decrees otherwise.

No other man in the Bible was as beloved as David. God made him a great king and filled his life with much joy while he was in obedience. Yet when he fell into disobedience, the price was exacted. Even David had to suffer the consequences of his folly.

Most of us live our whole lives in the realm of God's permissive will. We like to think that His yes isn't a definite yes, and that His no isn't a definite no. If we can manage to convince ourselves of this fallacy, then we have cut ourselves off from God's blessing.

God has His perfect will for us. There is only one path to this destination, and that is the path of obedience. To know the Lord's perfect will for your life, you have to be in perfect obedience.

If you are in perfect obedience to God, then nothing can stand before you, for God Himself will take up your battle, and no man can stand against Him.

The lives of these patriarchs of the Bible show in graphic ways the importance of obedience to God and the results of disobedience.

I pray that the conclusion you will reach in reading this book is that the price we pay for our disobedience is much too high, while obedience is our reasonable sacrifice unto the Lord.

1
Abraham
(Genesis 12-25)

The life of Abraham is of great importance because he was chosen of God to become the father of a new spiritual race. Religious seeds were planted in the garden of his heart from which were to spring wonderful results in the church of the future. He would be the father of all nations, and not just the Hebrew people, but all the nations of the earth would be blessed through him, because through him would be coming Jesus the Christ, the Messiah.

Mankind descending from Adam became hopelessly corrupt. It was swept away in the flood, but once again man became arrogant, impious, and moral darkness overspread the earth as man returned to the same old habits that he had before the flood.

By Hebrew oral tradition, we have the belief handed down to us from the time of Abraham that God said, "Let Abraham be," and there was light. The light of the world, Jesus Christ, the Messiah, would be coming from Abraham. The Lord said, "Let Abraham be," and Abraham was called into existence by Christ. This is the profound saying of the Talmud. In many a beautiful legend, the rabbis recounted the story of how Abraham refused to walk in the way of the tower builders, and he broke away from the heathen who surrounded him and from the heathenism of his everyday life.

One of these legends says that in Abraham's early childhood, one night, he looked at the stars under the clear Mesopotamian sky and felt, "These are the gods." But then dawn came, and soon the stars could be seen no longer. The sun rose. "This is now my god," Abraham said, "and him will I adore." But then the sun set, and he hailed the moon as his god. When, in turn, the moon was obscured, he cried out, "This, too, is not god. There must be one who is the maker of the sun, the moon, and the stars. There must be someone who created them."

Having gradually reached the momentous conviction that the universe was the work of one supreme being, one god, who is the god of righteousness, Abraham endeavored to open up the eyes of others to the follies of idol worship and idolatry. He became the preacher of the true faith. This was his mission in life— to go out and preach the gospel that there is a living God, that there is a God who created the heavens and the earth.

In Abraham's father's house, the story continues, there stood one great idol and a large number of smaller ones. Abraham's father, Terah, an idol maker, went to the marketplace one day and sold a huge order of idols. In the meantime, Abraham had broken all the smaller idols and placed the hammer in the hand of the big idol. When his father came home to fill the orders, he said, "Abie, what happened already yet? They're all broken!" Abraham told his father, "They quarreled among themselves, and the big one thereupon took the hammer and shattered them all. Look," he said to his father, "the hammer is still in the big idol's hand."

His father answered and said, "But son, there is no life and power in them to do such things."

Then Abraham turned to him and asked, "But Dad, how, then, can you fall down and worship them and ask them to heal your afflictions and to bring you love, peace, and the joy that passes all understanding? How can you possibly worship them when you say they have no power or life in their hands to do anything? You created them in your own hands. They're your creation."

The message got through to Terah, and Abraham asked his father the question, "Why then do you serve them if there is no power within them? Why? Can they hear your prayer, when you call upon them?"

Then Abraham was hauled before Nimrod, the king of Babylon. He had Abraham cast into a fiery furnace, which is where we get the name of the city of Ur of the Chaldees. The name "Ur" means fire. Abraham was placed in the fire by himself, but there was someone seen in that fire with him. The Angel of the Lord was there, protecting him. He stood guard around him, and the fire did not touch him. The Angel of the Lord rescued him from the fire, and later on, when God called Abram, He reminded him, "*I am* the Lord God who took you up out of Ur of the Chaldees. I am the One who rescued you out of the fire. I am the One who stood by you. I'm the One who has never forsaken you. I have never failed you. I will never fail you. I'm always with you." So Abraham was called the idol wrecker, but he was the father of a people coming into being who would shatter all idolatry, because from him would come Christ Jesus. We see Abraham bringing forth the true religion, the true belief in a living God. And we are adopted sons of Abraham through Christ Jesus.

Abraham became the fire leader of a great spiritual hope. While living with his father in Haran, he received a message from the Lord calling him to separate himself from all his associations and go into a new country. He was promised divine favor, great prosperity, and that he should become a blessing to all the families of the earth.

In Genesis 12:1-4 the Lord said unto Abram, "Get thee out of thy country, and from your family, from your kindred, and from your father's house unto the land that I will show you. I want you to leave everything that you have and go."

How many of us could do this right now if the Lord

3

told us to do it? Leave your bank account, leave your business, your job, your car, all your material posses-sions, and go? And when you get there, God will tell you that you're there. How many of us could truly do that? If we could do that, then we are truly the sons of the living God.

Abram was obedient unto the Lord, but he had a tendency to be like you and me—flesh—and so he was also disobedient to the Lord. The Lord told him, "Don't take any of your family with you. Go by yourself. I want you alone."

There comes a time in your life and in my life that the Lord wants us alone, so that He can minister to us. Do you realize that? Sometimes he wants you and me just to be with Him alone. Alone with nobody else. Just Jesus and I. Jesus and you. Remember, you and Jesus Christ make a majority; nothing and nobody can stand against you. There shall not one man stand against you all the days of your life, as long as you stay in Jesus.

The Lord told Abram to leave his father's house and go unto the land that God would show him. Abram was obedient, the phenomenon of obedience was in ex-istence.

And God gave Abram a promise. He said, "I will make of you a great nation, I will bless you. I will make your name great, and you will be yourself a blessing. And I will bless them that bless you and curse them that curse you, and in you all the families of the earth shall be blessed." He promised Abram Jesus Christ the Messiah right then and there.

But in his obedience, Abram was also disobedient. He took Lot with him. The Lord did not tell him to take Lot. With Lot, there was going to be trouble.

When the Lord is specific, He is specific. When He wants us to be obedient, He wants us to be obedient in every particular. And He constantly says that obe-dience is better than sacrifice: "I don't want your sacrifices. I want your prayers, your praise, your ado-ration, your worship, but I also want your obedience."

Abram was seventy-five years old when he departed

4

out of Haran. After the death of Abram's father, he went from Haran to Sichem. And there the Lord appeared unto him, and Abram built an altar unto the Lord. Who appeared unto him? Jesus Christ appeared to him personally and spoke to him. He was with him in the fire, and He appeared to him now and said, "Unto thy seed will I give this land."

Then Abram went from Sichem to Bethel, and from there he removed unto the mountain on the east of Bethel, and pitched his tent, having Bethel on the west, and Ai on the east; and he built there an altar unto the Lord, and he called upon the name of the Lord. He called the name of the place Bethel, meaning "house of God."

Do you suppose Abram knew what name of the Lord to call upon? Did the Lord reveal His name to him when He appeared to him? Did He give him a name that he could pronounce? Is there a possibility that God was that ungracious, that unloving, that unmerciful that He left him with the unpronounceable name of YHWH like we have in our Old Testament of today? (When the German translator translated it into the Gutenberg Bible, he came up with the name Jehovah, but we have no such name as Jehovah.) It's YHWH, an unpronounceable name.

Or is it possible that the Lord revealed Himself as Jesus, and He said, "Any time you want to reach Me, call upon My name Jesus." Is it a possibility that He said, "Just mention the name of Jesus. There is power in My name. Call upon My name, and I'm there."

And Abram journeyed, going on still toward the south. And there was a famine in the land: and Abram went down into Egypt, not to stay there, but to sojourn there until the famine was gone.

And it came to pass, when he was come near to enter into Egypt, that he now said unto Sarai his wife, "Behold now, I know that you are a very fair woman to look upon, a good-looking woman. And it will come to pass that when the Egyptians will see you, they will say, 'This is his wife,' and they will kill me, but you they will keep alive."

Abram was seventy-five years old, and Sarai was sixty-five years old—no spring chicken. But Abram was concerned. The Lord had given him every promise in the book. He was holding the promises of God in his hand, but he was worried. He took his trust out of the Lord and put his trust in his wife.

Abram said to her, "I want you to do me a favor. Say, I pray thee, that you are my sister, that it may be well with thee and with me for thy sake, that my soul may live because of thee. (Not because of You, Lord, but that my soul may live because of thee, Sarai. The Lord gave me every promise, but I've rejected all the promises. I have taken my trust and my refuge and my care out of the Lord, and I now put my trust in you, Sarai. Tell the Egyptians that you are my sister.)"

Of course, Abram was rationalizing the whole thing: "I'm not really telling a whole lie; I'm telling only half a lie. Sarai's my half-sister—"

This was Abram's disobedience to the Lord. His trust should have remained in the Lord. The Lord had given him the promise, "Unto thy seed will I give this land." The minute He gave that promise, Abram *knew* that from himself and Sarai would come a seed who would inherit the Promised Land. He had absolutely nothing to fear. The Lord would be with him all the way. He did not have to have Sarai go into sin on account of him—he caused her to sin by telling a lie. This was his disobedience. This was the phenomenon of obedience and disobedience.

Sarai was taken and placed in the harem of Pharaoh, and the Lord performed a miracle of sealing all the wombs in the harem of Pharaoh so that he was not able to touch any woman. This was the divine protection of the Lord.

Then the Lord appeared unto Pharaoh, because Pharaoh was inquiring, "Is something wrong here someplace? I don't understand what it is, but there's something wrong." And the Lord commanded him to go and humble himself before Abram. The Lord said,

"The man is a prophet, and he will pray for you, and you will be healed."

Abram came up out of Egypt with great wealth, and he returned to Bethel because he wanted to find the Lord again. He knew he had sinned. He knew he had stepped out of God's perfect will into His permissive will.

Remember, the Lord will give you and me enough rope to hang ourselves if we want to. He lets us do whatever we want to do. We have free will. We have free choice.

And Abram went up out of Egypt, he, and his wife, and all that he had, and Lot went with him, into the south. And Abram was very rich in cattle, in silver, and in gold. How did he become rich? Because of his wife, Pharaoh had given them all sorts of riches.

And Abram went on his journeys from the south even to Bethel, unto the place where his tent had been at the very beginning, between Bethel and Ai; unto the place of the altar, which he had made there at the first. And Abram called there on the name of the Lord, and he said, "I repent, Lord. I am sorry. Forgive me of my sin." And the Lord was just and faithful to forgive him of his sin.

Of course, all that gold, and silver, and cattle that Abram had acquired in Egypt didn't hurt him at all. So, once again he's going to pull the same trick and the same stunt. He's going to revert back to flesh. He learned a lesson, but he's going to forget it.

If you and I don't learn a lesson the first time, the Lord will permit it to happen to us again. He'll put us through the same routine.

Abram pulled the same stunt on Abimelech, king of Gerar. He made Sarai lie again. She said, "He is my brother," and he said, "She's my sister." Again, we see the divine intervention of the Lord. He appeared to Abimelech in a dream at night, and said, "She is another man's wife. Don't you dare touch her."

Even while the Lord was blessing Abram with

divine protection for Sarai, the enemy was at work, permitting Abram to receive wealth from the hands of those who worshiped idols. The Lord had told him, "I'm with you in all things. I will bless you. I will multiply you. Those who bless you, I will bless. Those who curse you will be cursed." So he had nothing to worry about, nothing to fear. But he accepted the material wealth of Satan, the enemy. Pharaoh was an idol worshiper. Abram received his gifts, and it was implanted in his mind that he could pull the same trick on another king.

Then Abram removed his tent, and came and dwelt by the terebinths of Mamre, which is in Hebron, and there he built another altar unto the Lord. He was in a state of repentance. And as he built this altar unto the Lord, he spoke to the Lord and offered his sacrifice of praise and thanksgiving.

From Hebron, he went to Damascus, where he pursued the robbers who had taken his nephew captive in the battle of the kings. Abram rescued Lot and recovered all of his goods for him.

Now a very strange thing happened when Abram returned to Hebron. On his way back, he met a man by the name of Melchizedek. And he gave a tithe to Melchizedek, a tenth of everything that he owned. Why should Abram do this? Who was this Melchizedek?

The name Melchizedek in the Hebrew means "King of peace" and "King of righteousness." In the seventh chapter of Hebrews, the Holy Spirit further enlightens us as to who Melchizedek is:

For this Melchizedek is king of Salem, priest of the most high God, who met Abram returning from the slaughter of the kings, and blessed him.

Who blesses—the greater or the lesser? The greater one gives the blessing to the lesser one. Abram is holding all the promises of God, and yet Melchizedek blessed Abram.

Who is the king of Salem? And what city is Salem? Jerusalem. It's two Hebrew words. *Jeru,* city; *salem,* peace—city of peace. But Jesus says there'll be wars;

8

there'll be rumors of wars. We are not going to have peace in our time—not until the King of peace comes back in triumph.

Now we see Melchizedek being without father, without mother, without descent, having neither beginning of days, nor end of life. He is made like unto the Son of God, and who abides as a priest continually. And who is our priest who will abide continually? Jesus Christ Himself. He is the one whom Abram met, the one to whom Abram gave a tithe.

After these things, the Word of the Lord came unto Abram. Earlier, the *Lord* had appeared to him. Now, the *Word of the Lord* appeared to him in a vision, saying, "Fear not, Abram: I am your shield, your *mogen*. I'm shielding you from this point on. I have a fire around you. Nothing, no one, will ever hurt you."

And Abram said, "O Lord God, what wilt Thou give me, seeing I go hence childless, and he who shall be possessor of my house is Eliezer of Damascus? Behold, to me You have given no seed, and lo, one born in my house is to be my heir."

And behold, the Word of the Lord came unto him, saying, "This man shall not be your heir. But he that shall come forth out of your own bowels shall be your heir."

And then he took Abram up into outer space by His Holy Spirit, and He said, "Look now toward heaven and count the stars—if you are able to count them—for so shall thy seed be."

And Abram believed the Lord. And the Lord counted it to him for righteousness that he believed at his age that he could still trust in the Lord and bring forth a son—even though he was as good as dead and his wife had long gone past the age of menopause.

Abram believed when the Lord told him, "Take a look at all these stars. So shall your descendants be," but immediately after the Lord had shown him all the universe, all the stars, he and Sarai decided to take things into their own hands.

In Genesis 16 we read that Sarai had a handmaid, an

9

Egyptian whose name was Hagar. And Sarai said unto Abram, "Go in, I pray thee, unto my handmaid. It may be that I shall be builded up through her."

In orthodox Judaism, this would mean that Hagar would sit on the lap of Sarai as Abram went in unto her, and then, when it was time for the child to be born, Hagar would again sit on the lap of Sarai.

Were Abram and Sarai standing on the promise of the Lord? No. The Lord had said, "I will multiply you as the stars and as the sand—not through an Egyptian woman, not through a handmaid—through you and your wife will the blessing of all nations come."

Once more, disobedience had come in. And from this disobedience, we have the problem still with us today. This problem is four thousand years old. Ishmael was born—here come the Arabs. The Jews and the Arabs are brothers. They come from the same father. But there is not brotherly love between them.

So Abram went in to Hagar, and she conceived, and when she saw that she had conceived, her mistress was despised in her eyes. Sarai was an old woman, and Hagar was a young handmaid, pregnant by Abram. The old woman was nothing in Hagar's eyes, because she was going to bring forth Abram's son.

And Sarai approached her husband and said unto him, "My wrong be upon thee. What did you listen to me for? Why didn't you listen to the Lord your God? You're supposed to be the prophet and the priest in this house. God's been talking to you the whole time— He never talks to me. Why didn't you listen to Him?"

Sarai continued, "The Lord judge between me and thee to see who is right and who is wrong." Sarai knew that she was right, because Abram never should have listened to her. He should have stood fast in the Lord.

Now what is Abram going to do? Is he going to do the godly thing that he's supposed to do? No. He passed the buck and sent Hagar right back to Sarai. And Abram said unto Sarai, "Behold, your maid is in your own hand. Don't bother me with her. Do with her whatever is good in your eyes."

Sarai dealt very harshly with her. She took advantage of her. She actually abused her.

When Abram was ninety years old, the Lord again appeared to him and said unto him, "I am God almighty; walk before Me, and be thou wholehearted. No more shenanigans from this point on. I want your whole heart. I judged you righteous for trusting Me and believing Me, but from now on, no more taking things into your own will. You're now going to stay in My perfect will, not My permissive will, but My perfect will. And I will make My covenant between Me and thee, and I will multiply thee exceedingly." And Abram fell on his face. And God talked with him, saying, "As for Me, behold, My covenant is with thee, and you shall be the father of a multitude of nations. Neither shall thy name any more be called Abram, but thy name shall be called Abraham."

The Lord took the letter "h" out of the name Yahweh, and He put it in the name Abram and called him Abraham. He made him part and parcel of Himself, because from him would be coming Jesus Christ the Messiah. He did the same thing with the name Sarai. He took the other "h" letter out of His name and changed the name of Sarai to Sarah, that she would be a princess, that she would be the mother of Jesus Christ.

The Lord again appeared unto Abraham when he was ninety-nine years old, and He commanded him to circumcise himself and every male in his household as a sign of God's everlasting covenant with him. And Abraham was sitting there in his tent on the third day, hurting very badly, when two angels and the Lord appeared unto him. The minute the Lord spoke to him, Abraham was instantly healed, and he rose up out of his tent and ran to bring provisions for the Lord and the two angels.

The abomination of Sodom and Gomorrah had come up to the Lord because they were homosexuals, and homosexuality is about the greatest abomination you can present to the Lord. Therefore, the Lord was about

11

to destroy Sodom and Gomorrah and six of the plain cities.

Speaking to Himself about the matter, the Lord asked, "Should I let Abraham in on what I am about to do?" He answered Himself, "Yes, because I have known him since before he was conceived in the womb. I've known him to the end that he would raise his children to honor and praise the Lord. So I will tell him what I am about to do."

Then He told Abraham that He was about to destroy Sodom and Gomorrah, but He permitted Abraham to intercede in prayer for them and the other heathen cities. Abraham's nephew, Lot, was at Sodom. He had become a judge in Sodom and Gomorrah and had become very affluent in the salt business. He had never preached the Gospel, but Abraham was depending on Lot to have done something for the Lord.

So when Abraham spoke to the Lord, he said, "Shall the Lord, the judge of all the earth, now destroy the righteous with the unrighteous? Lord, perhaps there are fifty righteous people there. Will You then destroy the city for fifty?"

And the Lord said, "For fifty, I won't destroy it."

And then Abraham said, "How about if there's forty-five?"

And He said, "For forty-five, I won't destroy it." And Abraham continued to bargain with the Lord. From forty-five he went down to forty: "Lord, how about if there's only forty there?"

And the Lord said, "For forty, I won't destroy it." Then Abraham jumped to multiples of ten, and he said, "Lord, how about if there's only thirty that are righteous—would You destroy the city for thirty?"

And the Lord said, "For thirty, I won't destroy it."

"How about twenty?"

"For twenty, I won't destroy it."

Finally Abraham said, "I'll speak to the Lord one more time. I have taken it upon myself.

"Perhaps there are only ten—would You destroy the city for ten?"

And the Lord said, "I will not destroy the city for ten's sake." And the Lord went off; He went His way.

As soon as the Lord left off speaking to Abraham, Abraham returned unto his place, figuring he had outwitted the Lord. He could count them up. "I've got Lot in Sodom and Gomorrah; I've got Lot's wife, that's two. They have two children, that's four. They're engaged to be married; that's six. And surely, in the years that have passed by, Lot has won four souls for the Lord." So Abraham figured he'd outwitted the Lord. "I've got Him down to ten, and the cities are spared." But Abraham had miscalculated, and the cities were destroyed. Only Lot and his daughters were saved.

Why did the Lord permit Abraham to step out by faith and intercede for these people? To teach him intercessory prayer. To teach him always to love your fellowman as yourself. No matter how bad a man may be, the Lord still loves him, and He'll permit you to intercede in prayer for him.

In the New Testament, Lot was accounted righteous—according to the righteousness of Abraham. Because the Lord made a promise to Abraham, He saved Lot from the overthrow.

Later, Abraham went from Hebron to Gerar. And then the covenant was fulfilled as God promised him. He had said, "At the appointed time, when I come back, next year, I will keep My covenant. I will keep My promise, and your son will be born." He even told him the day, the place, and the hour. It wasn't going to be by accident, but at the exact appointed time, the son of the old covenant would be born. And that son of the old covenant, Isaac, would never be permitted to leave the Promised Land. He'd never go to Egypt. He'd never go elsewhere. He would be in the Promised Land because he would be the representation of Christ Jesus. He would be the one who would be laid upon an altar to be sacrificed.

Abraham went from Gerar to Beersheba. He made a covenant with Abimelech and then went from Beersheba to Mount Moriah, where he built the altar unto

13

the Lord. And Isaac was prepared to be offered as a sacrifice.

Isaac never opened his mouth except to ask one question: "Father, where is the lamb for the burnt offering?" And the Holy Spirit descended upon Abraham, and the Holy Spirit said, "The Lord Himself will provide the lamb for the burnt offering for the sacrifice." And the Lord Himself provided that sacrifice on Mount Moriah two thousand years later, just a few hundred yards away, when Jesus Christ went to the cross for you and me.

Now this was perfect obedience. This was the phenomenon of obedience, that Abraham would believe God and trust God that when He commanded him to sacrifice his son, he believed that after three-days' journey the Lord could and would perform a resurrection in Isaac as He did in Jesus Christ.

We could say, "Praise the Lord," to that, and we could say, "Thank You, Jesus, for going to the cross for me." And Lord, we give You the praise, and the honor, and the glory that You were faithful in obedience so the phenomenon of obedience could take place, that You sought it as a joy and a prize. In Jesus' precious name we pray. Amen. Praise the Lord.

2
Jacob
(Genesis 25-35)

No other Bible character represents more fully the conflict between the lower nature of man and the higher nature of man than Jacob. He began as a supplanter, a conniver, a deceiver, and was transformed into Israel's prince and ruler with God. One minute, he was with the Lord. Another minute, he'd be reverting back to his old self again, back to his flesh. Beginning on the downgrade, at times he rose to glorious heights, only to sink again into the sordid struggle for gain.

Jacob was out to gain whatever he could gain. He was bound by a spirit of lust. He wanted the birthright, the blessing that belonged to his brother. But he emerged at the very last upon the plain of triumphant faith in the Lord as the Lord appeared unto him and spoke to him. He gave Jacob the born-again experience, and from that point on, Jacob started being born again every day into a new life. He died every day daily to his flesh. He learned the lesson that you and I have to learn, that once we are born again, once we come to know Jesus Christ, we can't just sit back in our triumph and say, "Well, we've got it made; from this point on, everything is going to be easy." Jesus never said that. The New Testament never said that. It says to die to your flesh daily, to die to yourself daily. There's no other way.

No devout reader who has ever studied Jacob's career can ever doubt that he was a chosen instrument of God in spite of all his weaknesses. The Lord promised us that He would use weak vessels, the weakest of all, to confound the strong.

There are two key thoughts which throw light upon Jacob's history. One is the unhappiness produced by family trouble and polygamy. The Lord demanded, back in the beginning of Genesis, speaking through Adam, that a man shall leave his father and his mother and should cleave unto his wife, and they should become one flesh. He never said that man should cleave unto his *wives*. One wife.

Trouble comes in through polygamy. This fact is illustrated throughout Jacob's entire career. The Lord permitted him to receive not one wife, not two, but three, four. Four wives. And his life was full of misery and unhappiness. The four wives constantly bickered among themselves, constantly fought together. The children constantly fought, because Jacob caused the tears of Esau when he stole his birthright and his blessing.

In Jacob's early life is the beginning of his downgrade, when he cheated Esau out of his birthright.

One day Jacob was boiling pottage—lintel soup, or lintel stew, which we Orthodox Jews make until this very day—when Esau came in from the field faint with hunger. And Esau said to Jacob, "I beg of you, let me have some of that red lintel stew, for I am faint, and I am famished." (This is why his name was called Edom, which is red, because they were red lintels.)

Even in that day and age, they knew as they would know when God made it a commandment, "If your brother comes to you desiring or having a need of anything, you are to *give* it to him. You are not to sell it to him, you're not to lend it to him, you are to *give* it to him outright, because the Lord your God has given you this as a blessing, and He'll replace it for you many times over."

But Jacob answered, "If you want this food, and

16

you're that hungry—" Jacob seized the opportunity to connive Esau out of his birthright—"then sell me today your birthright, the right of the firstborn."

Esau said, "See here, I am at the point of death. What good can this birthright do to me?"

Jacob said, "Swear to me today that you are selling it to me," and he swore to Jacob, and he did sell him his birthright. Then Jacob gave Esau bread and lintels, and he ate and drank and rose up and went his way. Thus Esau despised his birthright and scorned it from that day forth. He despised it because he was weak enough to sell his birthright for a bowl of food.

How often do you and I sell our birthright, not for a bowl of food, but for whatever the price happens to be? How often do we sell out for something maybe a little bigger than a bowl of lintels? It might be a house, it might be a car. It might be where the grass looks greener on the other side of the fence. The enemy knows our price, how cheaply we will sell ourselves to him.

Esau despised what he had done. He knew that all he had to do was to stand. He was raised in the way of the Lord. How could he possibly go so bad? His father was Isaac, the son of the promise. He was the son of the man who would never be permitted to leave the Promised Land. Isaac was on his way down to Egypt when there was a famine, and the Lord told him, "No, you stay here in your circumstance, in the very area that I have placed you. I have given you the promises of Abraham. I now make the same promises to you, that this land is yours, that your descendants will be as the stars and as the sand of the sea. I will bless those that bless you, I will curse those who curse you, and through you all the nations of the earth will be blessed. Through you is coming Jesus Christ the Messiah.

"So now, what need is there to go down into Egypt? You stay here with Me, and I'll stay here with you. You depend upon Me, and I will supply all of your needs." God never permitted Isaac to leave the Promised Land.

17

Isaac and Rebecca had trained the two boys in the way that they should go. The Scripture tells us that if you do train the children in the way they should go, that if they depart for a season, they will always come back.

Why do we have a problem in releasing our children to the Lord? All we need to do is trust God and know that our children are a trust from the Lord. All we need to do is be obedient. This is where the phenomenon of obedience comes in, to raise them and train them and pull them up. The literal Hebrew words mean "to pull them up in the way that they should go." You've got to keep on pulling. Bring them up in the Scripture. Keep them grounded in the Word, and if they do depart, you have the assurance and the guarantee of the Lord that He will always bring them back. You need not worry, because Christ has them in the palm of His hand.

When Isaac was old, and his eyes were dim so that he could not see, he called Esau, his elder son, and said to him, "My son," and he answered, "Here I am." He said, "See here now, I'm old. I do not know when I may die. So now I pray you, take your weapons, your arrows and your quiver, your bow, and go out into the open country and hunt game for me, prepare me appetizing meat such as I love, and bring it to me that I may eat of it and give you my blessing as my firstborn before I die."

Rebecca heard what Isaac said to Esau, and when Esau had gone to the open country to hunt for game that he might bring it, Rebecca said to Jacob, her younger son, "See here! I heard your father tell Esau to go out and bring young venison."

Rebecca had been in on a secret of the Lord from the very beginning, when she was still carrying the two boys in her womb. The Lord had told her the younger would be served by the elder, the younger would be greater than the elder. So now she was going to help the Lord out, because He couldn't possibly do it all by Himself. She heard that Isaac was going to pass the blessing to Esau. Esau knew in the back of his mind that the birthright that he sold would be no good without the blessing. The birthright and the blessing must go together. If one had the birthright and the other one had the blessing, in reality, the one who received the blessing was the one the Lord would bless.

So Esau figured that although he'd sold his birthright, he'd still receive the blessing in the end time. He'd still come out all right. But he didn't reckon with the fact that the Lord had spoken to Rebecca and told her the younger one, Jacob, would be the greater. And Rebecca was planning to intervene—because the Lord did not know how to divinely intervene—and stop the process of this blessing going to Esau instead of to Jacob.

The blessing must pass from Isaac to Jacob, whom the Lord has chosen. So Rebecca told Jacob, her younger son, "See here! I heard your father say to Esau your brother, 'Bring me game; make me appetizing meat so that I may eat and declare my blessing upon you before the Lord before my death.' So now, my son, do exactly as I command you." She did not put it in the realm of anything else but a commandment, and he knew that he was to honor his father and his mother that his days might be prolonged upon the face of the earth. He could cheat his brother, but he had to honor his mother.

Esau, remember, was his father's boy, a man's man. He was a hunter, a boy that any father could be proud of. Jacob was a mother's boy. He stayed in the tent, and was with his mama constantly. She was a typical Yiddish mama; she liked that little boy hanging around her apron strings the whole time. Rebecca said to Jacob, "Go now to the flock and bring me two good, suitable kids, and I will make them into appetizing meat for your father—such as he loves. I know exactly how to cook it for him, even better than Esau knows how to cook it. I can disguise the goat meat so that it will taste and smell just like venison. It will be even better to him than the real thing, and when your father eats it, he will declare his blessing upon you before his death."

"But," Jacob said to Rebecca, his mother, "my brother is a hairy man, and I am a smooth man. Suppose my father feels me, and I will seem to him to be a cheat and an imposter? That will bring his curse upon me, and not his blessing."

But his mother said to him, "On me be your curse, my son. Only obey my word and go and fetch the kids to me."

So Jacob went, got the kids, brought them to his mother, and his mother prepared appetizing meat with the delightful odor that his father loved. Then Rebecca took Esau's best clothes and put them on Jacob. Because Isaac was blind, he would think Jacob was Esau, from the smell of a hunter upon his clothing. And Rebecca put skins of the kids on Jacob's hands and on his neck, because Jacob was a smooth man, and Esau was a hairy man. She knew that when Jacob greeted his father, his father would say, "Come here, my son, and let me kiss you." And he would feel the hair on his neck and on his hands. Jacob would feel just like Esau and smell like Esau, and he would receive the blessing. Rebecca didn't trust God to accomplish His purpose Himself.

When the savory meat and the bread which Rebecca had prepared were ready, she gave them to Jacob. He went to his father and said, "My father, here am I."

"Who are you, my son?"

And Jacob said to his father, "I am Esau, your first-born."

The voice sounded strange to Isaac. He was expecting Esau, but now he heard another voice. And Jacob said again to his father, "I am Esau, your firstborn. I have done what you told me to do. Now sit up and eat of my game that you may proceed to bless me."

And Isaac said to his son, "How is it that you found the game so quickly, my son?"

And Jacob said, "Because the Lord your God caused

it to come to me. He gave me the blessing, and I found it quickly."

Then Isaac said to Jacob, "Come close to me, I beg you, that I may feel you, my son, and know whether you are really my son Esau or not." So Jacob went near to Isaac, and his father felt him and said, "The voice is Jacob's voice, but the hands are the hands of Esau."

Isaac asked him one more time, "Are you really my son Esau?" and Jacob answered, "I am." Then Isaac said, "Bring it to me, and I will eat of my son's game that I may bless you." Jacob brought it to him, and he ate, and he brought him wine, and he drank. Then Isaac said, "Come near and kiss me, my son."

This was the final test—to feel his neck, to know whether it was hairy or smooth. And Jacob came near and kissed him, and Isaac felt of his neck and smelled of his clothing.

Jacob had passed every test, and Isaac blessed him and said, "The scent of my son is as the odor of the field which God has blessed, and may God give you of the dew of heavens and of the fatness of the earth and abundance of grain and new wine. Let peoples serve you, and nations bow down to you. Be master over your brothers, and let your mother's sons bow down to you. Let everyone be cursed who curses you and favored with blessings who blesses you."

As soon as Isaac had finished blessing Jacob, and Jacob was scarcely gone out from his presence, Esau came in from his hunting.

Esau prepared savory food. He brought it to his father. He told his father, "Arise, and eat of your son's game."

And Isaac, his father, said to him, "Who are you?"

And he replied, "I'm your son, your firstborn, Esau."

Then Isaac trembled and shook violently and said, "Who—where is he who has hunted game and brought it to me, and I ate of it all before you came, and I have blessed him? Yes, and he *shall* be blessed, because I felt the Holy Spirit descend upon me as I gave that blessing. And yes, the Lord will bless him, as I imparted that blessing to him. The Lord has given me the assurance to know he *will* be blessed."

When Esau heard the words of his father, he cried out with a great and bitter cry and said to his father, "Bless me, even me also, my father."

Isaac said, "Your brother came with crafty cunning and treacherous deceit and has taken your blessing." Isaac recognized exactly what had happened.

Esau said, "Did you not rightly name Jacob, 'the supplanter, the conniver, the deceiver'? Did you not give him the right name? For he has supplanted me these two times. He took away my birthright, and now he has taken away my blessing. Have you not still a blessing reserved for me?"

And Isaac answered Esau, "Behold, I have made Jacob your lord and your master. I have given all his brethren to him for servants. With corn and new wine have I sustained him. What then can I do for you, my son?" The tears were streaming down the face of Esau, and those tears were going to have to be answered for and paid for to the Lord. What Jacob had sown, he was going to reap. The Lord permitted him to reap it for twenty years and longer to bring him to a point where He could give him a born-again experience, because he was going to have to flee for his life to keep Esau from killing him.

Esau said to his father, "Have you only just one blessing, my father? Bless me, even me also, my father." And Esau could not control his voice—he wept aloud.

Then Isaac, his father, answered, "Your blessing and dwelling shall all come from the fruitfulness of the earth and from the dew of the heavens above. By your sword, you shall live and serve your brother. But the time will come when you will grow restive and break loose, and you shall tear his yoke from off your neck. In the fullness of time, Christ will appear, and when Christ does appear, you'll be able to accept the Lord Jesus Christ and be free from that yoke which has been placed upon you by your brother Jacob. In Jesus

Christ there is no male, no female, no Greek, no slave, no Hebrew, no Jew. We're all equal in Jesus Christ."

Esau could be free in the fullness of time in Jesus Christ, but now Esau hated Jacob because of the blessing with which his father blessed him, and Esau said in his heart, "The days of mourning for my father are very near. When he is gone, I will kill my brother Jacob."

These words of Esau, her elder son, were repeated to Rebecca, and she sent for Jacob and said to him, "Your brother, Esau, comforts himself concerning you by intending to kill you. Now my son, do what I tell you: Arise, flee to my brother Laban in Haran."

The minute we get into one sin, it's going to lead into another sin, and it's going to lead from one lie to another lie. This is a part of the phenomenon of obedience and the phenomenon of disobedience.

Both of them were conniving, the mother and the son. How would Rebecca explain this to Isaac, her husband? He would surely ask, "Where's Jacob? What happened to Jacob?" She would have to find a reason and an excuse why Jacob was not around while the old man was on his deathbed.

"So now, my son, do what I tell you. Arise, flee to my brother Laban in Haran. Linger, sojourn there, dwell with him for a while, until you've heard that your brother's fury is spent. When your brother's anger is diverted from you, he will forget the wrong that you have done him—

"Then," she said, "I will send and bring you back from there. Why should I be deprived of both of you in one day? My husband is dying, and now if my son, Esau, kills you, I'll be deprived of both of you in one day, and I will have to mourn for both of you at the same time. Why should I mourn both of you? My husband lived to be a good old age. Now you flee to my brother Laban, and I will be deprived of just one of you."

Then Rebecca said to Isaac—now here's the excuse, here's the rationalizing—"I am weary of my life because of the daughters of Heth. These wives of Esau that he married of the Hittites, they've made my life miserable. If Jacob takes a wife of the daughters of Heth, such as these Hittite girls around here, what good will my life be to me? I'm going to send Jacob to my brother Laban, back where I come from. I'm going to send him back there to my family, and he can get a nice, good, little Jewish girl there for his wife."

Isaac called Jacob, and blessed him, and commanded him exactly as his wife had instructed him: "You shall not marry any of the women of Canaan. Arise, go to the house of Padanaram of Bethuel, your mother's father, and take from there as a wife one of the daughters of Laban, your mother's brother. And God bless you and make you fruitful and multiply you until you become a group of people, until you become a congregation, until you become Israel."

Then Jacob fled for his life. He left Beersheba and went toward Haran. But on his way, something strange happened to him.

And he came to a certain place, and he stayed there overnight because the sun was set. Taking one of the stones of the place, he put it under his head, and he lay there to sleep, and he dreamed that there was a ladder set up on earth, and the top of it reached to heaven, and the angels of God were ascending and descending on it.

Jesus later said, "I am that ladder. The only way that you can reach God the Father is through Me. I'm the only connecting link with God." There's no way to God except through Jesus Christ.

Notice the order of angels. They were ascending and descending. They were not descending and then ascending. They were ascending first. When Jacob left home, the Lord went with him, and the angels went with him. And they were changing shifts, the first group going up and then another group coming down to escort him on his journey. These were the angels who would protect him all the days of his life, and the Redeeming Angel that he would testify to later on, the

Angel of the Lord, Christ Jesus. He would testify to his sons, saying, "He has been with me my entire lifetime, but I didn't know it. Jesus touched me from the very beginning. He had a purpose and a plan for taking that conniving and that arrogance and that deceit and that lying and that cheating out of my life. From the very beginning, the Lord was with me."

As Jacob lay down to sleep and saw the ladder, behold, the Lord—Jesus Christ Himself—stood over and beside him and said, "I am the Lord, the God of Abraham, your father, and the God of Isaac, and I will give you and your descendants the land on which you are lying, and your offspring shall be as the dust and the sand of the ground, and you shall spread abroad to the east, the west, the north, the south, and by you, and your offspring—meaning Jesus the Christ, the Messiah—shall all the families of the earth be blessed and bless themselves. Through you will come Judah, who will be the father of David, and from him will come Christ, who will be called the son of David." He would never be called the son of Abraham, or the son of Isaac, or the son of Jacob, but He would be called the son of David.

Then He gave him a promise, and He said, "Behold, I am with you, I will keep watch over you with care, with tender, loving care, and I will take notice of you wherever you go. I will bring you back to this land, for I will not leave you until I have done all which I have told you, until I have accomplished everything that I told you I would accomplish in your life. You will be a blessing, and through you, the blessings of all the people of the earth will come."

And Jacob awoke, and he said, "Surely, the Lord is in this place, and I did not know it, because I thought that I could find the Lord only in a church, or a synagogue, or a temple, but not out here on a rock underneath the stars. But surely, the Lord is in this place, and I did not know it." He was afraid and said, "How to be feared and reverenced is this place! This is none other than the house of God, and this is the gateway to heaven."

And Jacob rose early in the morning and took the stone he had put under his head, and he set it up for a pillar, and he poured oil on its top as he dedicated this stone. This was the oil of the Holy Spirit as he anointed the pillar where the Lord appeared to him. And he named that place Bethel, meaning "house of God," but the name of that city was Luz at first.

Then Jacob made a vow saying, "If God will be with me and keep me in this way that I go, and will give me food to eat and clothing to wear, so that I may come again to my father's house in peace, then the Lord shall be my God. And this stone which I have set up as a pillar shall be God's house, and all the increase that You will give me, I will give a tenth of it to You." Now this is a greater tithe. He knew, by the precedent set by his father Abraham when he gave the tenth to Melchizedek, the King of peace, the King of righteousness, that he was to give the Lord a tithe. But he gave the Lord a greater tithe: "I'm not only going to give You a tenth of what I *have,* but I know that You will keep Your promise and You will give me the increase, and I will give You a tenth of the increase."

Do you want to be increased in your income? Do you know what to do? Give the Lord ten percent of the increase that you want and see if the Lord does not fulfill this promise. Give Him an increase of exactly what you want your income to be. The Lord spoke through the prophet Malachi, the last prophet appearing upon the scene to Israel, and He said, "You can test Me, you can try Me, you can prove Me, and see if I don't open the windows of heaven and pour out blessings beyond your imagination. I will even protect you from that which devours your income, from that which takes up your income."

Jacob had the vision of the Lord and made a vow at Bethel. Then he arrived in Haran and saw Rachel. And when Jacob saw Rachel, the daughter of Laban, his mother's brother, and the sheep of Laban, his uncle,

Jacob went near and rolled the stone from the well's mouth and watered the flock of his uncle Laban. A miracle took place right there, because it ordinarily took a group of men to roll away the rock to water the sheep. The Lord gave Jacob the strength to do it by himself.

As soon as Jacob saw Rachel, he fell in love with her. She had great big beautiful brown eyes. (When he met her older sister, Leah, he despised her because she was weak-eyed, and she squinted all the time. He couldn't stand Leah at all.) Jacob kissed Rachel, and he wept aloud that he was back at his mother's family's ranch and everything was fine.

Then Jacob said to Laban, "I will work for you seven years for Rachel, your younger daughter."

The seven years went by as if they were seven minutes, seven days, as if the seven years were nothing, because Jacob loved Rachel so much. When the seven years had passed, Jacob went to Laban and said, "Give me my wife that I may go in unto her and consummate my marriage."

They had a big wedding ceremony that night—drink and festivities and everything else. It was dark when Jacob went into the tent to his bride. In the meantime, Laban had slipped Leah into the tent instead of Rachel. Jacob went in unto her in the manner of all the world between men and women, and he woke up the next morning and saw *Leah!* And he said, "Woe is me! How did I get stuck with this?"

Then he confronted Laban with the situation: "How come you did this thing to me? What did I ever do to you that you should deceive me this way?" (This was the master conniver speaking.)

And Laban made up a law right on the spot. He said, "Did you not know after all this time the laws of our land? The elder must be married before the younger. Didn't you know this? You should have known it. But go fulfill Leah's week of her marriage, her honeymoon. Stay with her for the week, and after the seven days are up, I'll give you Rachel—but then you have to promise to work for her seven years. We'll give her to you in advance; your credit is good with us."

Jacob agreed to work seven more years, and after the seven days were up, he had two women in his tent —two who hated each other. They were squabblers from the very beginning. The Lord allowed it to happen because Jacob was a conniver. The romance was spoiled by the deception concerning his marriage, and the long sordid struggle with the father-in-law and the jealousy between his wives.

After some time, Leah had borne Jacob three sons— Reuben, Simeon, and Levi. And after she had given birth to Levi, she again conceived and bore a son. As the Holy Spirit descended upon her, she said, "This time will I praise the Lord," and she called his name Judah and left off bearing.

Judah means "praise." Praises of the Lord would come through the tribe of Judah. All the nations of the earth would praise God through the tribe of Judah, because of Jesus Christ, the lion of Judah.

The reason the Lord was so gracious and so merciful to Leah is because she was hated, but she was obedient.

The Lord always pours out His love and His grace and His mercy on the one who is obedient.

Leah was obedient to her father. She was obedient to her husband. She was not part of the deception. Her father had commanded her, "Go into that tent. I'm going to take advantage of Jacob." Leah fulfilled the commandment of honoring her father by her obedience to him.

Leah knew she was hated. Rachel hated her. Jacob hated her. They made no bones about it. Jacob always considered Rachel the only wife he had.

When Rachel saw that she bore Jacob no children, she envied her sister and said to Jacob, "Give me children or else I die. I don't want to live anymore."

Notice the arrogance that was still within Jacob. He became very angry with Rachel, and he said, "Am I God? Am I in God's stead who has denied you chil-

28

dren?" Look at the difference between Isaac's attitude and Jacob's. Isaac's wife, Rebecca, was also barren, but Isaac never rebuked his wife. He never came against her. Instead, Isaac entreated the Lord—he went to the Lord in intercessory prayer for Rebecca, and she conceived. The Lord answered Isaac's prayer, but Jacob was too arrogant to pray.

So Rachel offered him Bilhah, her handmaid, just as Sarah had offered Hagar to Abraham. Following the Hebrew custom, Jacob went in unto Bilhah, who sat on the lap of Rachel. Later on, when Bilhah was ready to give birth, she again sat on the lap of Rachel that Rachel might be builded up through her.

Eventually, Jacob had six boys by Leah, and two by Rachel—Joseph and Benjamin—after God had opened her womb. He also had four boys by the concubines. Then he had Dinah. Twelve boys and one girl. The twelve became the twelve tribes of Israel. Later, they would go into captivity in Egypt as the Lord had promised Abraham.

In the last part of Jacob's life, there was an upward movement, as the divine call was given to him after twenty years. The Lord had blessed him in cattle and in all blessing, and He told him to go back to the Promised Land. Departing secretly, he was pursued by his father-in-law, Laban, who had discovered that his idols were missing. Rachel had stolen them, not for the purpose of worshiping them, but because the custom of the land was that whoever possessed the idols when Laban died could go into court and claim all the inheritance. Jacob's connivance had rubbed off on his wife, Rachel.

Jacob did not know that Rachel had stolen the idols. When Laban caught up with them and stated his grievance, he was permitted to search through all their belongings, but he didn't find the idols. Rachel had hidden them in her saddlebag upon the camel, but she said, "I'm sorry, Dad. I can't rise up, because it is after the manner of women with me. It is that time of the month—you'll have to excuse my not getting up." And so Laban didn't search the saddlebag upon which she was sitting.

Without knowing who had them, Jacob pronounced the death sentence upon whomever the idols would be found. He said, "With whomsoever these idols are found, they shall die." And Rachel did die, giving birth to Benjamin. As she gave birth to him, she knew she was dying, and she called his name Benoni, meaning "son of my sorrow." But the Holy Spirit descended upon Jacob, and he immediately changed his name to Benjamin, meaning, "son of my right hand."

In the future, the Lord would take the tribe of Judah, from which He would bring the Lion of Judah, and the tribe of Benjamin, and would put them together in the kingdom of Judah with Jerusalem as its capital. Saul of Tarsus would be coming from the tribe of Benjamin and would be the right hand of Jesus Christ, as Paul the apostle, the greatest evangelist the earth has ever seen, preaching the Gospel to the ends of the earth.

Paul's ministry would be a prison ministry. He would go in synagogue after synagogue, preaching the Gospel, and he would get whipped, beaten, scourged, and imprisoned. But wherever he went, he counted it all joy. He rejoiced in the Lord always. He said, "Wherever I go, Lord, I know that this is Your purpose. This is Your plan. I know You have done this for a perfect reason, and I'm willing to stand in that reason in the phenomenon of obedience to You, Lord."

3

Joshua

(Joshua 1-24)

The life of Joshua, the soldier of the Lord and successor of Moses, can be divided up into four parts. The first part is his early life and preparation for leadership.

Joshua was the son of Nun of the tribe of Ephraim (Num. 13:8, 16). He was a youth when he was chosen by the Lord to be Moses' minister (Exod. 24:13). Every minister needs another minister, and the teenager, Joshua, ministered to Moses, a man eighty years of age.

When Moses would leave the tent of revelation where the Lord revealed Himself in the pillar of cloud, where Jesus Himself spoke to Moses face to face, mouth to mouth, Joshua would remain in the tent. The Lord was preparing him for the mission that was ahead of him by filling his mind with the mind of Christ Jesus.

Joshua is first mentioned at the battle with Amalek where he led the forces of Israel (Exod. 17:9-10). Moses stood on the top of the hill while the battle with Amalek was taking place below. As long as Moses' hands were upraised before the Lord, praising God and thanking God, the people of Israel were winning the victory. But as soon as he put his hands down, the Amalekites, the enemy, prevailed, and Israel began to suffer defeat.

When Moses' hands became too heavy for him to hold up, two intercessors came, one of them to hold up his right hand, and the other one to hold up his left hand. One of the intercessors was Aaron, and Hur of the tribe of Judah was the other. They both uplifted the hands of Moses until the enemy was completely defeated.

We see Joshua leading the battle, but being victorious only while intercessory prayer was going up, while someone was praising God and worshiping Him, thanking Him for the victory as the victory was taking place.

This was all part of Joshua's preparation for leadership. As the servant of Moses, he accompanied Moses part of the way up Mount Sinai when the ten commandments were given (Exod. 24:12-13), and he also attended him at the tent of meeting (Exod. 33:11). Whenever Moses met with the Lord, Joshua was there ministering to him, and then the Lord would minister to Joshua.

Later on, Moses chose Joshua as one of the spies to be sent from Kadesh to view the land of Canaan (Num. 13:1-3, 8, 16). Twelve spies were sent out, and Joshua, having a right spirit with the Lord, brought back a good report. Because he had seen the Lord in spirit and truth, he brought back a right report, an honest report. It was not embellished, not exaggerated; it did not take away from what he had seen.

The Lord had promised the children of Israel that they were going into a land of milk and honey, and Joshua and Caleb believed God's promise.

Can you believe God's promise in the circumstances in which you find yourself today? Can you believe His promise of health in the affliction you have today? Can you believe in His supply in the financial need that you have today? Can you believe His help in the spiritual need that you have today?

All you have to do is turn to Him and say, "Lord, I need You right now. Jesus, I need Your help right now," and Jesus is there to answer you.

Joshua and Caleb presented the minority report. The majority report acknowledged that the land was a good land, but they did not believe God's promise. They stressed that the land was fortified, heavily armed, and that there were giants in the land. They said, in effect, "We cannot possibly go in, Lord, and take the land that You told us was ours. There is no way we can believe Your word."

They were disobedient, unfaithful, and the Lord says over and over again that obedience is better than sacrifice. If they had trusted Him, been obedient to Him, they could have gone in and taken the land. It would have been theirs. Because they were not obedient, the children of Israel had to wander for forty years. After the forty years, Joshua and Caleb were permitted to enter the Promised Land while all the other male adults of their generation, 602,000 of them, perished in the wilderness (Num. 14:6-30).

The second part of Joshua's life deals with his career as leader of Israel, moving in obedience to the Lord. He was divinely appointed and ordained as successor to Moses (Num. 27:18-23). And Moses called unto Joshua, and said unto him in the sight of all Israel, "Be strong and of a good courage: for thou must go with this people unto the land which the Lord hath sworn unto their fathers to give them; and thou shalt cause them to inherit it. And the Lord, He that it is that doth go before thee; He will not fail thee, neither forsake thee: fear not, neither be dismayed" (Deut. 31: 7-8).

After the death of Moses, the servant of the Lord, the Lord spoke unto Joshua, the son of Nun, Moses' minister, saying, "Moses My servant is dead; now therefore arise. Get yourself up; don't sit there and mourn. Moses is with Me. You have nothing to grieve or to mourn about. Get up out of your lethargy—I have resurrected you. Go over this Jordan, you and all this people, unto this land which I do give to them, even to the children of Israel. They don't deserve it, but I'm giving them the land. It is a gift from Me. My love, My

33

grace, and My mercy is being given to the children of Israel. I am faithful to My promise," saith the Lord. "I have made an everlasting covenant with them, even to the children of Israel, even to the murmurers, to the rabble-rousers, these complainers, these gripers —even to them, I do give the land because I have given My word."

He gave them the promise, "Every place that the sole of your foot shall tread upon, I have given unto you. You can claim it for Me, saith the Lord. You can claim it for Jesus Christ."

When we went to the wailing wall in Israel, we laid hands upon that wall, and we claimed it for Jesus Christ. And we said that from now on, every person who touches that wall will touch Jesus Christ, and the Holy Spirit will touch them, and they will come to know and love Jesus as their Messiah.

We will see miracles taking place because a whole group of us agreed and by faith laid hands upon that wall and claimed God's promise—every place that you put your foot upon, He has given it to you. All you need to do is receive it by faith. Be obedient to the Lord and receive it.

God spoke to Joshua saying, "From the wilderness and this Lebanon even to the great river, the river Euphrates, all the land of the Hittites, on to the great sea toward the going down of the sun, shall be your border. There shall not any man be able to stand before you all the days of your life."

Does Jesus give us that very same promise—"There shall not any man be able to stand before you all the days of your life," because you know you have Jesus with you? Does He say, "I will never fail you"? In every area of your life, "There's no failure in Me," says the Lord. The only failure comes in us.

Here is the fact of obedience. He said, "Be strong and of good courage," because you have the strength of the Lord to have the courage to receive God's promise. It takes courage to stand on the promise of the Lord. It takes courage to stand up and move out by faith and trust God for exactly what He said He would do. This was the disobedience of the people of Israel. No matter what He did for them, they never had the courage to trust the Lord for the next day. And Jesus tells us that if we are worrying about tomorrow, we are sinning. We are to trust Him for every tomorrow.

Joshua was to be obedient, believing that every place where he set his foot, God had already given him. Wherever he led the three million people, he was to observe and do according to all the law which Moses, God's servant, commanded him. "Turn not from it to the right hand or to the left hand, that thou mayest prosper whithersoever thou goest."

Do we want success in life spiritually, physically, mentally, and financially? What is it that the Lord tells us to do? To be strong in Him. The joy of the Lord is the strength of our life. Be very courageous, observe to do according to all the Scripture. He is the Living Word, the Logos. There is life in the Word. Turn not from Him, to the right or to the left, that you may have good success wherever you go, that you will be blessed in all things. Stay grounded in the word; keep your mind stayed on Jesus Christ.

If you meditate on the word of the Lord day and night, your mind is stayed on Him. In your going in and your going out, constantly speak about the Lord Jesus Christ. Keep on praising the Lord.

What is our greeting for one another? Not "Good morning," or "Good evening," or "How are you?" We say "Praise the Lord!" Our minds are stayed on Him.

Jesus promised us that we would come under attack. If we are going to follow Him, we will be persecuted for His name's sake. But be strong and of good courage. Don't be afraid. You have nothing to be afraid of, for the Lord is your life and your salvation. He has already promised that no man shall be able to stand before you all the days of your life. Nobody will be able to stand against you, not even Satan, his principalities, his powers, his evil spirits, because Jesus overcame

*him on the cross. The Lord your God is with you wher-
ever you go.*

When Joshua began his career as the leader of Israel, three supernatural events occurred, confirming
that the Lord was with him.

The river Jordan was at floodtide; it was the season
of its highest peak. But it divided for the passage of
the people of Israel as soon as the priests set their feet
in the water. The water that was coming down from
above was held back by the Lord. As the Israelites
passed through the Jordan, it was as if they were baptized again. They were baptized the first time when
they went through the Red Sea.

They had had complete deliverance, complete salvation, but when they got to the other side, the murmur-
ing, the griping, the complaining started all over
again. They ran up against some bitter water. They
said, "Lord, do we have to drink this bitter water?
Why did You take us out of Egypt?" And they forced
Moses to go to the Lord with their complaints, and He
turned that bitter water into sweet water. He continued to show His love and His grace and His mercy
even during the disobedience of the people of Israel.
But God was obedient unto Himself, keeping His
promise, His everlasting covenant.

The second supernatural event occurred after they
entered the Promised Land. The Angel of the Lord
appeared to Joshua outside the walls of Jericho and
gave him directions for the plan of attack upon the
city. And it came to pass, when Joshua was by Jericho,
that he lifted up his eyes and looked, and, behold,
there stood a man over against him with his sword
drawn in his hand.

What did Joshua do? He approached the man with
the sword. What did he have to be afraid of? Nothing.
Nobody. Because the Lord Jesus Christ was with him.
Joshua asked the man, "Are you for us or against us?
Are you for us or our adversaries?"

He said, "No, I am the prince of the host of the Lord.

I am now come. You are beholding Me in a huge picture as when I come later on."

This was the Angel of the Lord, the Redeeming Angel Himself, Jesus Christ, speaking to Joshua. (God lets us know that the Son and the Father are one and the Father and the Son are one, over and over again in the Old Testament.) Jesus said, "I am now come. I am here to speak to you face to face. I AM the Lord."

And Joshua fell on his face to the earth. And the prince of the Lord's host said unto Joshua, "Put off your shoes from off your feet, for the place whereon you stand is holy." Joshua did as he was told. The very same thing had happened with Moses at the burning bush. It was the same Jesus who met him there.

Now, Jericho was straitly shut up because of the children of Israel. None went out, and none came in. And the Lord said unto Joshua, "See, I have given unto your hand Jericho and the king thereof and even his mighty men of valor."

In the Old Testament, "a mighty man of valor" is a man who cannot be purchased with a price. Even the heathen had mighty men of valor, just as the people of Israel had them. In that day and age, you could buy a man for a price. Each man had his price. But the Lord said, "Even the mighty men of valor that cannot be purchased for a price, I have delivered into your hands. I, the Lord your God, have given you the entire city.

"And ye shall compass the city, all the men of war going about the city once. You shall do this six days. And seven priests shall bear seven rams' horns before the ark. I, Myself, will go before you, and the ark of the covenant with the ten living words, the ten commandments. And on the seventh day, you shall compass the city seven times, and the priests shall make a long blast with the rams' horns. When you hear the sound of the horns, all the people shall shout with a great shout. 'Hallelujah! Praise the Lord!' And the wall of the city shall fall down flat."

Now there were two sets of walls surrounding Jericho. The inner walls fell down toward the city—flat. There was only one house saved. That was the house of Rahab, the harlot. She was saved by the blood of the Lord, she and her entire household, because she had that scarlet cord hanging down from her window, the scarlet cord which represented the blood of Jesus Christ.

She believed. She had asked the question of the two spies, "Whom can I save?" And they had said, "As many as you can get in your house. She had that house packed with people. She saved her entire household because she was obedient to believe God's word.

Whenever we are obedient to the Lord, the Lord will be obedient unto us. Now it's hard for us to think that the Lord will be obedient unto us. First of all, He's obedient unto Himself. He is faithful unto Himself. He makes a promise, and you can rest assured in that promise. You never have to worry or fear that the promise will not take place.

The inner walls fell inward; the outer walls fell outward. They formed a bridge that every man should go up exactly as the Lord had stated. That was the third miracle.

The first miracle, the River Jordan divided; the second miracle, the Angel of the Lord appeared; the third miracle, the people gave a signal, and the walls of the city fell flat, opening the way for a complete victory.

Joshua met with only one reverse. The only time he suffered defeat was at Ai, teaching the necessity of absolute obedience to God's commands.

Joshua didn't understand why they had suffered defeat. So to whom did he go? Did he gripe to the people? Did he gripe to himself? No, he went directly to the Lord, and he said, "Lord, why? Why will You now permit the heathen to say that You brought up this people over Jordan to destroy us?" He used the same intercessory prayer that Moses used once before with the Lord. "Would You have those who do not know You say that You couldn't take care of Your people?"

And the Lord told Joshua, "There is an accursed thing in the camp. You have put gold and silver before Me, before your worship of Me, and this has come between you and Me," saith the Lord. "If you get rid of the accursed thing, I will be with you once again."

Somebody had to confess it, somebody had to repent to the Lord—but nobody came forth to repent. Nobody confessed to the sin.

Then the Lord said to Joshua, "I want you to assemble all three million of the people of Israel tomorrow, and I will choose the guilty party."

The Lord help us when we reach that point that the Lord Himself has to accuse us before we come to Him. He says, "I'll give you every opportunity to retrace your evil steps, to repent, to come to Me to find forgiveness, salvation, love, grace, mercy." This way was open for the guilty family, but they would not come forward.

The Lord said, "Call them all to stand before Me, and I will choose." And He called the family of Zerah, of the tribe of Judah, and the family of Achan, and He said, "Now you step forward; you're the guilty party." And Achan admitted to his sin, but it was a little bit late, because now the Lord had to glorify Himself before all the people of Israel, and He passed judgment upon Achan's entire family. They were all stoned to death, as the Lord commanded, by the people of Israel. And then they were burned with fire to cleanse the people of Israel.

The Lord said, "I am a devouring fire." Jesus said, "I will baptize you with fire." John the Baptist said, "I baptize you with water, but there's one who comes after me who will baptize you with the Holy Spirit and with fire." We do have to go through a fire in our lives as the Lord refines, and cleanses, and burns the chaff out of our lives as He did here with the people of Israel.

Achan's disobedience caused the entire defeat at the battle of Ai, but from this time forward, when the people of Israel stood up and were obedient to the Lord, carrying out God's command in regard to the family of Achan, Joshua went steadily onward until he had dethroned thirty-one kings. And the greater portion of the land was subdued.

The next thing Joshua did was to divide the land among the tribes as he was commanded by God. Those who had a greater number of people in their tribe received a greater inheritance; those who had a smaller number of people in the tribe received a smaller inheritance. And the Levites did not receive an inheritance in the land. The Lord said to them, "Your inheritance is in Me," but He commanded the people of Israel to take care of His ministers, His Levites, His priests. He said, "I have caused them to stand by faith, so I will place the burden upon you to take care of them. Don't ever let any Levite want or lack because he trusts Me."

Part three of the life of Joshua in his obedience to the Lord, the phenomenon of obedience, is in his last days. Before he died, he delivered a farewell address to Israel in which he counseled the people of Israel to be loyal to God and remain a separate nation.

They had made a covenant—that was Joshua's other failure—when the enemy came disguised as a people from a faraway land, wearing old clothes, carrying stale bread and polluted water. They said, "We've traveled a great distance. So now make a covenant with us."

The question was asked of them, "How do we know that you are not the enemy that the Lord our God has commanded us to drive out from before us?"

They said, "Well, take a look at the evidence. Take a look at our clothes. Don't they look like we came from a faraway land? Take a look at our bread—it's stale. Take a look at our water—it's polluted."

They looked at the surface, and they didn't look underneath, and they made a covenant with the people of the land, although the Lord had said, "You shall not make a covenant with them. You shall not have anything to do with them. You shall drive them out from before you. Otherwise, they will become a thorn in your side. You will be as they are. You will be worse than they are, and as I thought to do unto them, I will do unto you, because you will pick up their abominable practices."

But Joshua was deceived, and he made a covenant with the people of Caanan, allowing them to live, although the greater commandment was the Lord's command to drive out all the nations from before them, to destroy all the heathenism, all the idolatry, all the sorcery, all the witchcraft, all the people.

Before Joshua's last days were up, he commanded the people to be loyal to God and remain a separate nation. He said, "Now we have the Cananites among us. We have the enemy among us. Satan is among us, but remain separate."

This is the same message that Jesus said: "You can live in the world but not be a part of it." This is the same thing Joshua was telling the people of Israel. "You can be in the world but not be a part of it."

Know that the Lord your God is with you. Jesus is with you always, never leaving you nor forsaking you, and He will never fail you. When the enemy does attack, call upon the name of Jesus, because there is power in the name.

The fourth part of Joshua's life is the conquest that the Lord caused him to be a part of as they went in and conquered the land. The conquest was a type, a picture of the battle of the Christian life as we see the Christian fighting with the triune forces of evil. Just as we have God the Father, God the Son, and God the Holy Spirit, Satan has a counterfeit. The triune force of the enemy is the world, the flesh, and the devil—Satan himself.

We constantly have to fight the world; we constantly have to fight our own flesh; and we constantly have to fight Satan himself, because he's ever attacking the people of Jesus Christ, and we stand in Christ knowing that we are victorious in Him, that the Lord is our life.

He is our salvation. He is our deliverance, and we have nobody or nothing to fear. We stand victorious.

Joshua's victory was won by faith. He trusted in the Lord by faith. He believed His Word. He was obedient unto the Word of the Lord.

The same thing is true in your life and my life. We can overcome our foes. Every Christian can overcome his foes; in Jesus Christ, you are an overcomer. You will always be victorious.

The fruit of the conquest was soon lost by Joshua's successors. Why? They surrendered to their old enemies, the flesh, the world, and the devil.

The same thing can happen to you and me today. We are victorious in Jesus Christ. He did win the victory for us. He did give us the battle. He did go before us. He did bear our sin, our transgression, and our iniquity, our afflictions, our griefs, and our sorrows. And by His stripes, we are healed. The victory is complete, but then sometimes we do like the people of Israel—we go back and surrender to the triune forces of evil.

Rest, the peace of God, comes only to those who maintain the position they have won. Jesus says He is our rest. We are to rest in Him. "Be still and know that I am God; stand still and see the salvation of the Lord."

Can we stand still and see the salvation of the Lord? Can we rest in Jesus Christ and know that He is Lord, that once He has given us His promise, His promise is faithful, and just, and true?

He is the everlasting covenant. He did cleanse us from everything, and we stand victorious in Him. And as the enemy comes upon us—the world, the flesh, and the devil himself—we can stand.

The Lord says, "No man shall stand against you, or come against you, or be able to stand before you all the days of your life as long as you remain standing with Jesus Christ, knowing that He is with you always."

This is our position now. This is where we stand, in

Jesus Christ. And everyone of us can become an over-comer.

I know there are many Christians reading these words who have needs. Your need can be surrendered to Jesus Christ. And as you surrender it to Jesus Christ, leave it with Him—don't ever pick it up again. Leave it with the Lord.

You're not the burden-bearer. I'm not the burden-bearer, but Jesus is the burden-bearer. He says, "I will take all burdens from you. I will lift them all from you, because I have been lifted up, and as long as I am lifted up, I'll draw all mankind unto Me. And I'll take your sin, I'll take your transgressions, your iniquity, and the chastisement necessary for you to receive your peace which passeth all understanding. Already, I took it all upon Myself. By My stripes, you were healed in every area of your life."

Praise the Lord!

4

Gideon

(Judges 6-9)

We saw the phenomenon of obedience in the life of Joshua, that as long as he lived and the remaining of his elders lived, Israel remained faithful to the Lord. When the last of his elders died and he died, Israel started to sin all over again. Again they rejected their heavenly Father, the Lord who delivered them out of slavery, out of bondage, out of captivity.

In every situation, God always provides. By His love, and His grace, and His mercy, He always sends a messenger. He always sends a prophet. He always sends somebody who'll bear the good news. And in this case, He picked Gideon, of one of the half tribes of Israel. The two tribes of Manasseh and Ephraim were each considered half a tribe, because they both descended from Joseph.

Gideon, the mighty man of valor, was the son of Joash of the tribe of Manasseh. In his day, Israel had forsaken God, was in abject condition, terrorized by the Midianite robbers who desolated the country and made life intolerable.

As usual in times of distress, Israel repented and cried unto the Lord. God was faithful and just to accept their repentance, and He sent them a prophet to rebuke the sinful people. The purpose of the rebuke was that they might turn from their evil ways and once more seek to do the will of their heavenly Father.

*When we are sinning, God will always send some-
body to rebuke us, to reprove us. Usually, He Himself
will speak to us first about our sinfulness. If we refuse
to listen to Him, He will speak to us through our
spouse, if we have one. He or she will begin to rebuke
us. That's exactly what God wants our mate to do. If
you don't listen to the voice of your mate. He may send
your best friend to speak to you. And if you still don't
hear, He will send somebody else. He keeps trying to
reach you, trying to call you back to the right path, to
the path of salvation, to the way, the truth, and the
life.*

God issued a call to Gideon to deliver his nation. He
sent His angel to summon Gideon to leadership. But
Gideon didn't consider himself a leader, and so he pro-
tested against God's call. He had no education, his
family was poor, and he himself was the least in his
father's house. Even his tribe was considered just half
a tribe.

But the Lord didn't listen to his excuses. Instead, He
assured him, "I will go before you. I will do the deliver-
ing. I will do the saving. I will show you how to attack
the enemy. You don't have to do a thing except be obedient to what I tell you to do."

The Angel of the Lord (in the Old Testament, the
Angel of the Lord, the Redeeming Angel, is Jesus
Christ Himself) appeared unto Gideon and said, "The
Lord is with thee, thou mighty man of valor."

And Gideon said unto him, "Oh my Lord, if the Lord
be with us, why then is all this befallen us? Why have
You forsaken Israel?"

God had forsaken Israel because they had refused to
hear His voice. He had warned them that if they for-
sook the Lord, they would be delivered into the hand
of the enemy. The Lord would remove His divine protection, and the shekinah glory of God would depart
from Israel, leaving them open to attack. It had come
to pass.

*The same thing happens in a Christian life. If we
willfully and deliberately sin, we grieve the Holy Spir-*

it, and He will leave us. He cannot dwell in an unclean and unholy temple. But praise God, He loves us enough that He convicts us of our sin, and returns to us when we repent and pray, "Lord, forgive me of my sin."

Jesus never leaves us. Even while we are backsliding, while we are still in sin, Jesus says, "I am with you always. I am with you while you're doing the right thing, and I'm with you when you're doing the wrong thing. Once I get you in My hands, nothing, nobody, can ever take you out."

Jesus said, "Father, all that You have entrusted to me, I have kept in Your name. I have not lost any except the son of perdition, Judas Iscariot. The rest I will never lose. I am the Good Shepherd. My sheep know My voice. And as they know My voice, they follow Me."

One of the excuses that Gideon used against the Lord was that the Lord had forsaken Israel. "Why are You then bothering Israel? Why are You bothering with me? Pick somebody else. I'm not Moses. Moses gave You four excuses. I am going to use three."

Gideon's excuse was, "I'm not fit for the task. I've had no training. I don't know anything about leading people. I can't speak."

Then the Lord gave him a promise, assuring him that the divine presence, the Holy Spirit of God, would be with him, and then He gave him another guarantee. He said, "I will give you a guarantee of a certainty of success, and I will even give you a supernatural sign to encourage your faith."

But Gideon said unto Him, "Oh my Lord, wherewith shall I save Israel? Behold, my family is the poorest in Manasseh and I am the least of my father's house."

And the Lord said unto him (here's the guarantee), "Surely I will be with thee. You shall smite the Midianites as one man."

And Gideon said unto Him, "Now if I have found favor in Your sight, then show me a sign." The typical Hebrew attitude, always asking for a sign. Constantly, the apostles with Jesus Christ said, "Lord, give us a sign."

Gideon wanted a supernatural sign. He said to the Lord, "Don't leave me. Don't depart from here until I do something, I pray Thee. Please Lord, don't depart until I come unto Thee and I bring forth my present."

If we want something from the Lord, do we have to bring Him a present? Is that what the Lord said He wants? He said, "I want the prayer and the praise of your lips and of your heart. Obedience is better than sacrifice." He wanted Gideon to be obedient.

And the Lord spoke to Gideon, saying, "I will tarry. I will wait until you come back."

And Gideon went in, made ready a kid and unleavened cakes of an ephah of meal; the flesh he put in a basket; he put the broth in a pot; then he brought it out unto Him under the terebinth (the turpentine tree) and presented it.

And the Angel of God said unto him, "Take the flesh and the unleavened cakes, and lay them upon this rock, and pour out the broth. Pour it above the whole thing."

And he did so.

Then the Angel of the Lord, Jesus Christ, put forth the end of the staff that was in His hand, and He touched the flesh and the unleavened cakes; and there went up fire out of the rock, and consumed the flesh and the unleavened cakes. Then the Angel of the Lord departed out of his sight.

Here was the miracle. It was like the sacrifice of a burnt offering. The Holy Spirit now consumed the entire offering, and Gideon knew for a certainty that it was the Lord who spoke to him. This was the supernatural sign he was looking for.

This encouraged his faith and his obedience in stepping out and believing God for what He told him he can do in the Lord. By himself, Gideon could not do it. He could not deliver Israel.

We come now to the events leading up to the battle with the Midianites.

The Lord said unto him, "Peace be unto thee; fear not, you shall not die. Don't be afraid. I am Your divine protection. Now do as I tell you what to do." Then Gideon built an altar unto the Lord, and called it Jehovah-shalom, "The Lord is my peace." Unto this day, in Ophrah of the Abiezrites, that altar still stands.

The greatest gift that Jesus gave us when He left this earth was to say, "I leave My shalom with you. I leave My peace with you, not as the world knows it, but My peace."

Gideon destroyed the altar of Baal, and the groves (Hebrew, *asherah,* a phallic symbol, a male sex organ that the people of Israel worshiped as they picked up the abominations of the heathen).

After Gideon had destroyed the asherah, cut them down, he was threatened with death by the idolaters. His father had a choice to make. He could stand up for idolatry, or he could stand up for the Lord and his son.

They said one to another, "Who has done this thing?" And when they inquired and asked, they said, "Gideon, the son of Joash, has done this thing." Then the men of the city said unto Joash, "Bring out your son that he may die, because he has broken down the altar of Baal, and because he has cut down the *asherah* that was by it."

And Joash said unto all that stood against him, "Will you contend for Baal, or will you save him? Is it proper that you stand up and protect a god that you worship? Can you protect your god? Can you protect your Baal?"

Can you and I protect Jesus Christ? Can you and I defend Him, or is He our defense? This idol that you worship, can you now defend him? If he is a god, let him defend himself.

Joash made a choice. He stepped in between the idolaters and his son to protect his son, because he knew as he came back to the Lord in his heart, that the Lord would grant him the protection that he needed.

Joash said, "He that will contend for Baal shall be put to death before morning. If he, Baal, be a god, let him now protect himself. He doesn't need your protection because one has broken down his altar."

Gideon's father had rescued him from the idolaters, because now he was standing with the Lord. On the assembling of the host of the enemies, Gideon blew a trumpet and called all of Israel together.

Now all the Midianites and the Amalekites and the children of the east assembled themselves together, and they passed over and pitched in the valley of Jezreel. But the Spirit of the Lord clothed Gideon. He was completely engulfed by God's Holy Spirit. He blew a horn, and Abiezer gathered together after him. And he sent messages throughout all of Manasseh, and they also were gathered together after him. He sent messages unto Asher, unto Zebulun, and unto Naphtali, and they came up to meet him.

Two encouragements and a severe test came to Gideon before he made his attack upon the enemy. First, his faith was strengthened by the sign of the fleece. He felt it necessary to ask for a sign again from the Lord. The Lord had answered one sign already. He had assured him of the victory. He had assured him of the success, as the Holy Spirit consumed the offering, but Gideon wanted to test the Lord one more time.

*Is it wrong for Christians to set a fleece before the Lord? No, I don't see anything wrong with it at all, but remember that a fleece has to be in the realm of the miraculous, something that cannot happen except by the divine intervention of the Lord.**

Gideon spoke to the Lord and said, "I will put a fleece of wool on the threshing floor. If there be dew on the fleece only, and it be dry on all the ground, then I shall know that You will save Israel by my hand, as You have spoken."

Gideon rose up early the next morning to see if the Lord had honored the fleece. He pressed the fleece together and wrung enough water out of it to fill a bowl full of water.

*For a modern-day example of a fleece, see Appendix 1.

And the ground around the fleece was completely dry, just exactly as Gideon had asked the Lord that it would be to prove God's will to him.

But Gideon wasn't quite satisfied yet, not quite ready to stand by faith, to be obedient. He said, "I believe You, Lord, but—God, let not Your anger be kindled against me, but I will speak just one more time. Let me make trial one more time, I pray Thee. Just this one more time with the fleece—let it be dry only upon the fleece; and upon all the ground, let there be dew."

And it was so. Everything was covered with dew. The fleece was totally dry.

The Lord had given Gideon the sign that he needed to strengthen his faith so that he could walk in perfect obedience. The phenomenon of obedience was about to take place.

Gideon's faith was going to be severely tested by the reduction of his army. The Lord told him to call an army together, and he gathered thirty-two thousand men. Then the Lord told him, "The people that are with thee are too many for Me. I cannot give the Midianites into their hands, lest Israel vaunt themselves against Me. They will take the praise and the honor and the glory from Me and say, 'We did it ourselves.'"

The gracious thing about the Lord is that He constantly comes back and says, "Come back to Me, My children, and I will love you. Come back to Me, and I will forgive you. I have already accomplished everything for you upon the Cross of Calvary. I took your griefs, your afflictions, your sorrow, your sins, your transgressions, your iniquity. The chastisement necessary for you to obtain your peace, I took upon My back, and by My stripes you were healed in every area of your life."

The Lord told Gideon, "Now, therefore, make proclamation in the ears of the people saying, 'Whoever among you is fearful, whoever is frightened, whoever among you is trembling, let him return and depart early from Mount Gilead."

How many people were afraid? How many people departed? Take a look: And there returned of the people twenty and two thousand. They went back home, afraid and trembling because the Midianite army far surpassed them in numbers. There were a hundred and fifty thousand Midianites, and only ten thousand Israelites left.

But the Lord said unto Gideon, "The people are yet too many. Bring them down to the water, and I will try them. They won't have to stand inspection for you; they will have to stand inspection for Me. I will now give the roll call, and they will stand before Me. I shall try them there for you, and it shall be of whom I say unto you, 'This shall go with you,' the same shall go with you; and of whomsoever I say unto you, 'This shall not go with you,' the same shall not go."

So he brought down the people unto the water, the ten thousand, and the Lord said unto Gideon, "Every one that lappeth of the water with his tongue, as a dog lappeth, him you shall set by himself; likewise, every one that bows down his knees to drink." And the number of them that lapped, putting their hand to their mouth, were three hundred men: but all the rest of the people bowed down upon their knees to drink water.

The Lord picked the three hundred men who lapped the water like an animal, like a dog. Why? Those who bowed down upon their knees to drink were in the habit of bowing down to Baal. The minute they got to the water, they knelt and they drank the water. But the others were not in the habit of kneeling to Baal, because in Hebrew worship we don't kneel, we don't bow, we prostrate ourselves before the Lord, and then we lift up our hands in worship and in praise. The Lord said, "I will take the three hundred who drink of the water like a dog. Those are the ones I want."

And again, Gideon was mystified. "Are You going to deliver Israel with just these three hundred men, Lord?"

And the Lord said unto Gideon, "By the three hundred men that lapped the water will I save you." The word "save" or "salvation" means Jesus. "By these three hundred men will I let you see My Jesus. He will go before you. And I will deliver the Midianites into your hands. Let all the other people go, every man back to his own place. Just keep the three hundred men."

It came to pass the same night, the Lord said unto Gideon, "Get yourself down upon the camp of the enemy, for I have delivered it into your hand." But Gideon needed another sign from the Lord. How many signs would it take for him to believe what had already been accomplished? The Lord said, "It's already been done. Go down and take it." But knowing the heart of Gideon, God told him, "If you now fear to go down, go down with Phurah your servant down to the camp." (The name *Phurah* in Hebrew means "deliverance.") "Go down now with your servant to the camp, and you shall hear what they say, and afterward shall your hand be strengthened. You will receive the joy and the strength of the Lord as you will now receive another sign from Me to do what you have to do to be obedient."

So Gideon went down with Phurah his servant to the outermost part of the armed men that were in the camp. Now the Midianites and the Amalekites and all the children of the east lay along the valley like locusts in multitude, and their camels were without number, as the sand by the seaside.

And when Gideon was come, behold there was a man telling a dream unto his fellow, saying, "Behold, I dreamed a dream and, lo, a cake of barley bread tumbled in to the camp of Midian, and it came unto the tent, and smote it that it fell, and it turned upside down and the tent lay flat."

And his fellow answered and said, "This is nothing else save the sword of Gideon, the son of Joash, a man of Israel. Into his hand, God hath delivered Midian and all the host."

This was the sign that Gideon needed, the one to which the Lord had referred when He said, "I will strengthen you as you receive an additional sign. I will again prove Myself to you." When Gideon heard the telling of the dream and the interpretation thereof, he worshiped the Lord. And he was made ready to move out, by the phenomenon of obedience, and be obedient unto the Lord.

Gideon returned to the camp of Israel and said, "Arise. What is it that you're doing? You're lying down on the job. Arise. The Lord said we are to go in and take the land. Let us take the victory. It is ours. Arise, for the Lord has delivered into your hand the host of Midian."

Then the Lord gave Gideon the plan of attack. How do you attack a hundred or a hundred and fifty thousand men with just three hundred?

The Lord, being a good general, said, "Here is what I want you to do. Divide the three hundred men into three companies, a hundred men on each side of the camp, to surround it, and put into their hands horns and empty pitchers, with torches in the pitchers."

Then Gideon said to the Israelites, "Look unto me and do likewise, and behold, when I come to the outermost part of the camp, it shall be that as I do, so shall you do. When I blow the horn, I and all that are with me, then you blow the horns also on every side of the camp and say, 'The sword of the Lord and of Gideon!'"

So Gideon and the hundred men that were with him came unto the outermost part of the camp in the beginning of the middle watch, when they had but newly set the watch—they had just changed shifts. The Israelites blew the horns, broke in pieces the pitchers that were in their hands, and held the torches in their left hands and the horns in their right hands wherewith to blow, and they cried, "The sword of the Lord and of Gideon!" They did exactly as the Lord told them to do.

What will happen if we are obedient to the Lord? The deliverance will take place. The victory is assured. The victory is complete.

And they stood, every man in his place round about

the camp, and all the host of Midian ran, and they shouted, and they fled. And they blew the three hundred horns, and the Lord now set every man's sword against his fellow. Israel did not have to pick up one sword or destroy one Midianite. The Lord did it all. He took the swords of the Midianites and turned them against each other. They killed each other. The terror of the Lord was upon them.

If the Lord is for you, who can be against you? And if the Lord is against you, there is nobody that is for you.

The Lord now was against Midian. He had held out salvation to them for thousands of years, and they had refused it. Judgment was now passed upon the Midianites.

And the Lord turned sword against sword, and they destroyed each other as the terror of the Lord came upon them. And the Lord set every man's sword against his fellow, even throughout all the hosts, and the host fled as far as Bethshittah toward Zererath as far as the border.

When the Lord visited the camp of the foe, the victory was complete. The uniqueness of the plan of attack of the Lord was perfect, and the defeat of the Midianites was overwhelming because the Lord let it be. He laid the plan; all the Israelites had to do was to be obedient to the Lord.

Something strange happened before Gideon died. He was offered the crown of Israel: Then the men of Israel said unto Gideon, "Rule thou over us, both you and your son and your son's son also, for you hath saved us out of the hand of Midian." Had Israel learned a lesson? Who had saved them? The Lord had saved them. But they said, "Now you, Gideon, be king over us. You rule us, because you're the one who saved us out of the hand of Midian."

But Gideon said unto them, "I will not rule over you, neither shall my son rule over you. The Lord shall rule over you. He is your king. As long as you turn to Him, your deliverance, your salvation, your need is assured, the victory is assured, the victory is complete. All you have to do is lean on Him, cleave unto Him, and rest in Him."

But as he made the statement giving the honor and the praise and the glory to the Lord, once again, Gideon wanted to give the Lord a present.

And Gideon said unto the Israelites, "I would make one request of you, that ye would give me every man the earrings of his spoil." They had spoiled the Midianites, taking gold, silver. They had gold in the earrings, because they were Ishmaelites.

And they answered, "We will willingly give them." And they spread a garment, and they did cast therein every man the earrings of his spoil. And the weight of the golden earrings that he requested was a thousand and seven hundred shekels of gold besides the crescents and the pendants, and the purple raiment that was on the kings of Midian, and besides the chains that were about their camels' necks.

And now Gideon made an ephod thereof, and put it in his city, Ophrah. An ephod was a garment the high priest wore.

The ephod was made of gold, as a tribute and a memorial to the Lord. This was the present Gideon was going to present to the Lord.

But all Israel went astray after it, and it became a snare unto Gideon and unto his house. It became a snare to all Israel. They worshiped the ephod—this thing that they made by their own hands. They were back into their old habits, into their old trap. Satan had come in and attacked them through their giving a gift to the Lord.

The Lord didn't ask for a gift. All He asked for was obedience. He did not command Gideon to make an ephod. He did not command him to do anything except to lead the battle and be there.

Gideon judged Israel, and he lived to a good old age, but the snare and the trap was there as the people worshiped that ephod. And that ephod had to be destroyed like the brazen serpent had to be destroyed.

Remember the brazen serpent in the wilderness?

The people of Israel sinned. The Lord sent serpents upon the children of Israel. As they were bitten by the serpents, they were dying by the thousands, and the Lord told Moses, "If the people of Israel would believe—take two crossbeams, put them together, and take a serpent made out of brass—which represented sin—and lift it up on the hill, and if the people of Israel would look up and look past that brazen serpent and look to Me, they will be healed of their wounds, and they will not die."

The people of Israel who believed looked at the brazen serpent, looked beyond it, looked to the Lord, and they were healed. Those who did not believe, died of their snakebites. But then as they came in from the wilderness into the Promised Land, they took the brazen serpent with them. It ended up in the sanctuary of the Lord. They gave the brazen serpent a heathen name, Nehushtan, and they worshiped it for a long time, even at the time of King David. It was not until Hezekiah that the brazen serpent was destroyed, because it had become an object of worship.

As Christians, we don't worship the cross, but we worship who was upon it. The cross is empty. The resurrection took place. Without the resurrection, we are nothing.

So the people of Israel missed the point entirely with the brazen serpent. It is the emblem of the medical profession until today, the caduceus. When the people of Israel looked up, they were healed by the Lord, but then they started worshiping the object itself. And this is what they did with this ephod until it was destroyed.

So now, the phenomenon of obedience is the fact that God expects us and wants us to remain obedient to Him. He has shown us the way. He has shown us the truth. He has shown us the life. And if we walk in the way, and the truth, and the life, what is that He says He will do for us? "Every place that you set your foot upon, I will give it to you. You will have good success in everything that you touch and in everything that you do."

Praise the Lord!

5

Samuel

(I Samuel 1-15)

Samuel was about the only judge in Israel whom you could call an upright judge. Now the Hebrew word for judge doesn't mean a judge sitting behind the bench. In Israel, a judge was a prophet of the Lord, one who was sent by God. As people brought their grievances to him, he took them to the Lord in intercessory prayer.

Samuel had a godly mother.

The greatest ministry that the Lord can give any human being on the face of the earth is to be a mother. If the mother is a godly woman, the son will always be a godly man. We have evidence to prove this—every king of Judah who had a godly mother was a righteous king before the Lord. All nineteen kings of Israel, every one of them worse than the other, had heathen mothers, even though they had Israeli fathers. Where the mother brings up a child in the nurture and the admonition of the Lord, the child walks with God. Where he's brought up in idolatry, he walks in idolatry.

Women have the greatest ministry that God can give any human being on the face of the earth. The child sees the father very little. He's out earning a living for the family. He's out doing what he has to do, but the mother is the one who implants the seed of faith in the heart of that child.

Samuel had a godly mother, Hannah, and he was born in answer to her prayer when she was in distress of soul, praying to the Lord and weeping bitterly. She vowed, saying, "O Lord of hosts, if you will indeed look upon the affliction of your handmaid and earnestly remember and not forget your handmaid but will give me a son, I will give him to the Lord all his life, and no razor shall touch his head."

She took a Nazirite vow for her son before he was born. He would not eat grapes. He would not touch the fruit of the vine. No razor would touch his head. The Nazarite vow was a total dedication to the Lord.

The name Hannah in Hebrew means, "She upon whom the grace of the Lord rests."

Hannah had the grace of the Lord upon her, and the Lord answered her prayer and gave her a son. She named him Samuel, which means, "the Lord has heard."

When she had weaned him, she took a three-year-old bull, an ephah of flour, a bottle of wine to pour over the burnt offering for a sweet odor unto the Lord, and brought those things with Samuel to the Lord's house in Shiloh to be trained by the priests.

Then they slew the bull and brought the child to Eli, and Hannah said, "Oh my Lord, as your soul lives, my Lord, I am the woman who stood by you here praying to the Lord. As I made a vow unto the Lord, He accepted the vow, and He permitted Himself to be entreated of me. For this child I prayed, and the Lord has granted my petition made to Him.

"Therefore, I have given him to the Lord. He was given to me as a trust, and as long as he lives, he is given to the Lord. I will never step in between him and the Lord. He belongs to the Lord."

Hannah's unfailing love caused her to make Samuel a little coat and to take it to him every year as she went up to worship the Lord at Shiloh, coming with her husband to offer the yearly sacrifice.

The yearly sacrifice was a sacrifice of atonement, a sacrifice of repentance as commanded in the book of

Leviticus. One time during the year, they were to go up and worship the Lord and prepare themselves ten days before the Day of Atonement. They were to prepare their hearts, prepare their souls, and examine themselves to see that they were right with the Lord before they brought the sacrifice of atonement before the Lord, that they might be made one with Him, forgiven of their sins, their transgressions, and their iniquities.

As Hannah took Samuel a little coat, he knew he was loved, not just by his heavenly Father, but also by his earthly father and mother. This was the sign of love that Samuel needed.

A dear pastor friend of mine was always out on the road evangelizing and ministering as his little boy was growing up. When he came home at night, he would go into the room where the little boy was asleep, and he would tie a knot in his sock. When the boy got up in the morning, he knew that his dad had taken the time and trouble to go in and tie a little knot in his sock, telling him that he loved him. This was the sign of love that he needed.

Samuel had a very remarkable boyhood. The phenomenon of obedience had already been brought into being in his life by his mother's obedience to the Lord. Samuel ministered before the Lord while he was still a child, a child girded with a linen ephod. He was dressed as a priest of the Lord.

The high priest, before he could go into the holy of holies on the Day of Atonement, had to put off his priestly garment, with his crown, with his miter. He had to go in dressed in a simple linen garment, as Jesus went in a simple garment without sin to be your high priest and my high priest.

Jesus had a crown of thorns upon His head, and the blood dripped down His face. And when He went to the cross, He died in His own fluids. It was a horrible way to die. But He took that affliction upon Himself so that you and I wouldn't have to suffer.

Samuel had what is regarded by many as the most

wonderful call to religious service of any boy in the Bible: Now the boy Samuel ministered to the Lord before Eli. And the Word of the Lord was rare and precious in those days.

There is coming a day in this country when the Word of the Lord is going to be rare and precious. You're not going to have meetings like you're having now. We're going to see things we never dreamed of before, because the enemy is pouring out his spirit as God is pouring out His Holy Spirit. The enemy knows his time is very short. He knows he's already been defeated on the cross by Jesus Christ, and he knows Christ is on His way back. So he's pulling out all the stops. The first thing the enemy does is that he tries to come against the Word of the Lord—we saw it happen in Germany, we saw it happen in Spain, we saw it happen in Syria. When the enemy rises up like a flood, he tries to take away the living Word of Jesus Christ because Christ is the Word.

So in those days in Israel, the Word of the Lord was rare and precious, and there was no frequent or widely spread vision. The Lord was not communicating with the people of Israel, because they were so deep in sin, and nobody wanted to hear the Word.

At that time, Eli, whose eyesight had been so that he could not see, was lying down in his own place. The lamp of God had not yet gone out in the temple of the Lord. This is a verification of what Josephus wrote later on, that when Christ was born, the lamp of God went out in the temple, because the light of the world, who was Jesus Christ, came into the world, and there was no longer any necessity for the lamp which was lit in the tabernacle to remain lighted.

When the Lord called Samuel, he ran to Eli, and he said, "Here I am. Why did you call me?"

Eli said, "I didn't call you. Go back and lie down." So he went back, and he lay down. He's still a child, remember.

And the Lord called again, "Samuel."

And Samuel arose and went to Eli and said, "Here am I; you did call me."

Eli answered, "I did not call, my son. Lie down again."

Now Samuel did not yet know the Lord, and the Word of the Lord was not yet revealed to him. Samuel had not seen the revelation of Christ Jesus as yet. He was still a little boy, but the Lord was calling him. He had called him to his ministry while he was still in the womb of his mother; even before he was conceived, she had made a vow unto the Lord, and the Lord answered her prayer. It was foreordained, known by God, that Samuel would be a prophet of the Lord and an upright judge before all of Israel.

And the Lord called Samuel the third time, and he went to Eli and he said again, "Here I am. You did call me."

Then Eli, who was a high priest, perceived that the Lord was calling the boy. And Eli said to Samuel, "Go, lie down, and if He calls you, ye shall say, 'Speak, Lord, for Your servant is listening.'"

So Samuel went and lay down in his place. And the Lord came and stood right by him. And He called him as at the other times, "Samuel, Samuel."

When the Lord speaks to you, He always calls you by name. When He spoke to me, He called me by name, saying, "Michael, Michael."

Then the child Samuel answered, saying, "Speak Lord, for Your servant is listening."

Then the Lord told Samuel, "Behold, I am about to do a thing in Israel at which both ears of all who hear shall tingle. Their ears have been plugged up, but I'm about to do something in Israel that they'll not only hear, but their ears will tingle. On that day, I will perform against Eli all that I have spoken concerning his house from beginning to end, and I now announce to him that I will judge and punish his house forever for the iniquity of which he knew, for his sons were blaspheming God, bringing curses upon themselves, and he did not restrain them."

61

What was the sin of Eli, the high priest? His sons, who were priests, one of whom would replace Eli as high priest, had made themselves vile. They were having sexual relationships with women in the sanctuary of the Lord, the women who were coming in for counsel. That is why the Word of the Lord was rare and precious in those days. The high priest, Eli, had closed his eyes to the whole thing, and he hadn't reprimanded the boys.

The Lord promised judgment to Eli and to his family. He said, "I have placed you here as a shepherd, as a pastor—you are My high priest. You have caused My people to sin, and because you did not restrain your sons, therefore, I have sworn to the house of Eli that the iniquity of Eli's house shall not be atoned for or purged with sacrifice or offering forever." The Lord said, "I have passed you from grace into judgment. I will not accept your sacrifice. I will not accept your atonement. I will not accept your offering forever, because I have spoken to you by My Holy Spirit. You have rejected, you have refused. You have been disobedient. I have spoken to you over and over again, and you have closed your eyes to the whole situation. You did not want to hear. You have blasphemed My Holy Spirit. I will not listen to you from this point on."

The Lord told all of this to Samuel, and He said, "This shall come to pass."

Samuel lay until morning. Then he opened the door of the Lord's house, and he was afraid to tell of what he heard to Eli. Eli was the high priest, and Samuel was just a little kid. He didn't want to tell Eli the judgment of the Lord.

But Eli called Samuel. He was interested in knowing what the Lord had to say to Samuel. He said, "Sammy, come here. What did the Big Boss have to tell you, because the Big Boss hasn't been talking to me lately. What did He have to say to you?"

So Eli called Samuel and he answered, "Here I am." Notice his obedience. "Here I am. I'm ready to speak to you."

Eli said, "What is it that He told you? Pray, do not hide it from me. God do so to you, and more also, if you hide anything from me of all that He said to you. I want to know all the facts—everything."

And Samuel told him everything, hiding nothing. And Eli said, "It is the Lord. Let Him do what seems good to Him." Eli knew he had been passed from grace unto judgment, and he surrendered to the Lord, saying, "It is the Lord. It is the Lord's judgment. I accept the judgment, and now let the Lord do what seems good to Him."

In Samuel's mature years, the Lord gave him special revelations, and he became a prophet.

Samuel grew, and the Lord was with him, and He let none of his words fall to the ground, that is, none of the words the Lord gave Samuel ever came back void nor empty. They were planted, as seeds to bring forth harvest.

That same promise holds for you and me, that if we go out and plant a seed, or we preach the Gospel, or we witness to somebody about Jesus Christ, He gives us the assurance and the guarantee that His Word will never come back void nor empty.

All Israel from Dan to Beersheba knew that the Lord had established Samuel, while he was still a child, to be a prophet of the Lord. And the Lord continued to appear in Shiloh, for the Lord revealed Himself to Samuel in Shiloh—in the Word of the Lord. In Jesus Christ, He revealed Himself as God the Father and God the Son. That is how He appeared to Samuel.

After the death of Eli, Samuel became prophet and judge in Israel. Some time after the return of the ark by the Philistines, he assembled the people of Israel at Mizpeh. He called upon them to repent of their idolatry and turn to the God of Abraham, Isaac, and Israel. Then Samuel said to all the house of Israel, "If you are returning to the Lord with all your hearts, then put away the foreign gods and the ashtaroth from among you." They had been worshiping the sex god and sex goddess. "Direct your hearts to the Lord and serve

Him only, and if you serve Him only, in obedience, He will deliver you out of the hand of the Philistines."

If you are living in the wilderness right now, try being obedient unto the Lord. He will deliver you today—right now, He will deliver you. The deliverance is there, because it's been accomplished on the cross. Jesus accomplished it all for you and me. The deliverance is complete, final, once and for all.

We die to our flesh daily, that which has not been crucified, that which has not been surrendered to the Lord, that little part that we're still clinging to in our flesh. That's the part of us that has to die daily. But He died for us once and for all.

The Israelites listened to the Word of the Lord, spoken through the prophet and the judge Samuel. They put away the Baal and the ashtaroth and served the Lord only.

Hearing of the assembly of the Israelites at Mizpeh, the Philistines gathered together to make war against them. When the Israelites heard of it, they were afraid of the enemy. After all the miracles they had witnessed, they were still afraid of the Philistines.

And the Israelites said to Samuel, "Do not cease to cry to the Lord our God for us. Continue, Samuel, to pray to the Lord our God for us, that He will save us from the hand of the Philistines. We have repented. We are serving the Lord. We have gotten rid of the Baal. We have gotten rid of the ashtaroth. We are obedient unto the Lord, and the phenomenon of obedience is taking place. So you continue praying unto the Lord that He will be with us, that He will save us—that He will 'Jesus' us, that Jesus will be with us."

So Samuel took a suckling lamb, and offered it as a whole burnt offering to the Lord, and Samuel cried to the Lord for Israel, and the Lord answered him. As Samuel was offering the burnt offering, the Philistines drew near to attack Israel, but the Lord thundered with a great voice that day against the Philistines and threw them into confusion, and they were defeated before Israel. They slew one another. Israel did not have to lift her hands. The Lord was before them.

And we do not have to lift our hands, because Jesus is our defense. If we are obedient unto the Lord, He goes before us. He is with us always. He is the One who does the fighting for us. We can't save anybody. We can't save ourselves, but He is our Savior. He's our deliverance. He's the One who saves us.

And Samuel judged Israel all of his days. And he went from year to year in circuit to Bethel, Gilgal, to Mizpeh, and he was judge for Israel in all those places. Then he would return to Ramah, for his home was there, and there he judged Israel, and there he built an altar unto the Lord.

In his old age, Samuel made his first mistake.

We are bound to make mistakes, because we are flesh and blood. We walk close to the Lord, but once in a while, we have a little bit of our flesh to which we haven't yet died.

Samuel had a little part of his flesh to which he hadn't yet died. He saw himself getting older, and the Lord had not yet appointed another judge over Israel. So when Samuel was old, he took God's job upon himself—he appointed his sons judges over Israel.

Now the name of his firstborn was Joel; the name of his second Abiah; they were judges in Beersheba. And his sons did not walk in his way, but they turned aside after the other gods that Jesus says you cannot worship. He says you can worship either the Lord your God or mammon. Mammon is the evil word for money. And Samuel's sons turned aside after gain. They took bribes and perverted justice, and they broke the commandment of the Lord in their disobedience.

All the elders of Israel now assembled and came to Samuel at Ramah. They said to him, "Behold, you are old, and your sons do not walk in your way. Now appoint us a king to rule over us like all the other nations." The wickedness of Samuel's sons made the people demand a king.

They had been lusting after a king ever since they

left Egypt. They wanted to be like all the rest of the nations. They did not believe that God was able to grant and to fulfill the promises that He gave them. They saw every miracle take place, but they still did not believe. The phenomenon of obedience was there, but yet the other phenomenon of disobedience was still much with them.

So they said, "Make us a king. Why shouldn't we have a king who would ride out in a golden chariot with horses and trumpets blowing, and we can have pomp and ceremony? Give us a king."

The Lord, being God, being omniscient, had warned the people of Israel way back in Moses' farewell address. He said, "There is coming a day when you're going to reject Me as your King, and you're going to ask for yourself an earthly king, and I'm going to let you have him. But I'm going to tell you what this earthly king is going to be like. I'm going to give you fair warning far in advance. You want to step out of My perfect will, and I'll let you. You want to be in My permissive will, and I will let you go. But you know what My perfect will is. I am the only God. I am the only Father. I'm the only King that you have."

Israel's desire for a king was really a rejection of the Lord, and Samuel tried in vain to dissuade them from their decision. He told them all the words of God's warning: "These will be the ways of the king which shall reign over you. He will take your sons; he will appoint them for his chariots, and to be his horsemen, and some shall run before his chariots. He will appoint them to be commanders over thousands and over fifties; he will have them plow his ground; he will have them reap his harvest; and make him implements of war and instruments of his chariots. He will take your daughters to be perfumers, cooks, and bakers. He will take your fields. He will take your vineyards. He will take your olive orchards, even the best of them, and give them to his servants.

"He will take a tenth of your grain and your vineyards and give it to his officers and to his servants. He will take your men. He will take your women servants and the best of your cattle and your donkeys and put them to work. He will take a tenth of your flock, and you shall be his slaves. And in that day when all this comes to pass that the Lord has warned you about, you will cry out because of your king you have chosen for yourself, but the Lord will not hear you then."

Nevertheless, the people refused to listen to the voice of Samuel, and they said, "No, we will have a king over us, that we also may be like all the other nations, and that our king may govern us and go out before us and fight our battle. We reject the King who threw all that confusion and terror into the Philistines so that we didn't even have to raise our sword, but they slew themselves. We want an earthly king who will go before us in battle and who will fight for us."

Can you think of a better champion than the Lord? Somebody who will go before you so that you don't have to gain the victory yourself, but He will grant you the victory? There is none but the Lord.

So Samuel was obedient unto the Lord as the Lord told him to anoint Saul. Samuel took a vial of oil and poured it on Saul's head and kissed him and said, "Has not the Lord anointed you to be prince over His heritage Israel?" He didn't make him a king. He made him a prince. God was still King. He remains King over Israel and over His people for all time, for all eternity.

After Samuel had anointed Saul, he gave him some instructions: "When you have left me today, you will meet two men by Rachel's tomb in the territory of Benjamin at Zelzah; and they will say to you, 'The donkeys you sought are found, and your father has quit caring about them and is anxious for you, asking, "What shall I do about my son?"'" Then you will go from there, and you will come back by the plain of Tabor, and three men going up to God at Bethel will meet you there, one carrying three kids, another carrying three loaves of bread, another carrying a skin bottle of wine. They will greet you. They will give you two loaves of bread which you shall accept from their hands; and after that, you shall come to the hill of God where the garrison of the Philistines is, and when you come to the city, you will meet a company of prophets coming down from the high place with harps, tambourines, a flute, and a lyre before them. They shall be prophesying. They shall be speaking in an unknown tongue. They are prophets of the Lord. The way you will know them is that you will hear them coming down, singing in the Spirit.

"As you hear them, something will happen to you, Saul. The Spirit of the Lord, His Holy Spirit, will come upon you mightily, and you will show yourself to be a prophet with them, and you will be turned into another man. You will have a born-again experience as you now become as they are, and you will sing and pray in the Spirit as they do.

"When these signs meet you, do whatever you find to be done, for God is with you. You shall go down before me to Gilgal; and, behold, I will come down to you to offer burnt offerings and to sacrifice peace offerings. You shall wait seven days until I come to you and show you what you shall do."

And when Saul had turned his back to leave Samuel, God gave him another heart. And all those signs came to pass that day. And when all who knew Saul beforehand saw that he spoke by the inspiration of the Holy Spirit among the school of prophets, then the people said one to another, "What is come over him? Who is he? He's nobody but the son of Kish. Is Saul among the prophets?"

When Saul had ended his inspired speaking, he came to the high place. Saul's uncle said to him and to his servant, "Where did you go?"

And Saul said, "To look for the donkeys, and when we found them nowhere, we went to Samuel."

Saul's uncle said, "Tell me, what did Samuel say to you?"

Saul said to his uncle, "He told us plainly that the donkeys were found." But of the matter of the kingdom of which Samuel spoke, he told him nothing.

Then Samuel called the people together to the Lord at Mizpeh. There he said to the children of Israel, "Thus saith the Lord God of Israel: 'It was I who brought you up out of Egypt and delivered you out of the hands of the Egyptians and out of the hands of all the kingdoms that have oppressed you. It was I who brought you up. Nobody else. But you have this day rejected your God who Himself saved you from all your calamities and your distresses, and you have said to Him, "No. Set a king over us." So now present yourselves before the Lord by your tribes and by your thousands.'"

And when Samuel had caused all the tribes of Israel to come near, the tribe of Benjamin was taken by lot. And when he had caused the tribe of Benjamin to come near by their families, the family of Matri was taken, and Saul the son of Kish was taken, but when they looked for him, he could not be found. Therefore, they inquired of the Lord further if the man would yet come back, and the Lord answered, "Behold, he has hidden himself among the baggage." They ran and brought him from there, and when he stood among the people, he was a head taller than any of them.

And Samuel said to all the people, "Do you see him whom the Lord has chosen, that none like him is among all the people?" And all the people shouted and said, "Long live the king."

Then Samuel told the people the manner of the kingdom. He again reminded them of what the Lord had told them of the king in relationship to God and the people, and he wrote it in a book and laid it up before the Lord. (It was the Book of Samuel that we read today.) Then Samuel sent all the people away, each one to his own home. Saul also went home to Gibeah, and there went with him a band of valiant men whose hearts God had touched. But the children of Belial said, "How can this man save us?" They despised him and brought him no gifts. But he held his peace.

And Samuel said to all of Israel, "I have listened to you and all that you have said to me, and I have made a king over you. You have asked for a king; the Lord granted permission. And now behold, the king walks before you. I am old, and I am gray, and behold, my sons are with you. I have walked before you from my childhood to this day. I have done everything in my power that I thought was right before the Lord. I made one mistake—I appointed my sons as judges and prophets over you. But the Lord rebuked me for it, and I have repented of this to the Lord. Whose ox or whose donkey have I taken? Have I ever taken a bribe from you? Whom have I defaulted or oppressed, or of whose hand have I received any bribe to blind my eyes? Tell me, and I will restore it to you."

And they said, "You have not defaulted us. You have not oppressed us. You have not taken anything from any man's hand. Your faith, your dependence, your trust has been in the Lord always. He has supplied all of your needs.

And Samuel said unto them, "The Lord has witnessed against you, and His anointed is witness this day, that you have not found anything in my hand."

And they answered, "He the Lord is witness."

And Samuel said to the people, "It is the Lord who appointed Moses and Aaron and brought your fathers up out of Egypt. Now present yourselves that I may plead with you before the Lord concerning all the righteous acts of the Lord which He did to you and to your fathers."

Samuel told Saul, "The Lord sent me to anoint you king over His people Israel. Now listen and heed the words of the Lord. Thus saith the Lord of hosts, 'I have considered, and I will punish what Amalek did to Israel, how he set himself against them in the way when Israel came up out of Egypt. Now go and smite Amalek and utterly destroy all that they have. Do not spare them, but kill both man and woman, infant and suckling, ox, sheep, camel, and donkey. Don't spare anything.

"I want you to be obedient. Kill them all. The infants are dedicated to temple prostitution. The males are dedicated to homosexuality. Spare none of them."

So Saul assembled the men and numbered them at Telaim, two hundred thousand men on foot and ten thousand men of Judah. All came to the city of Amalek and laid wait in the valley.

Saul warned the Kenites, "Go, depart, get down from among the Amalekites, lest I destroy you with them, for you showed kindness to all the Israelites when they came up out of Egypt." So the Kenites departed from among the Amalekites.

And Saul smote the Amalekites from Havilah as far as Shur that is east of Egypt. And he took Agag, king of the Amalekites, alive although the Lord had said, "Spare no one." And he destroyed all the rest of the people with the sword.

Saul and the rest of the people spared Agag and the best of the sheep. Did the Lord tell them to spare the sheep or the oxen? No. He specifically said to kill everything. But they took the best of the flock; they spared the king and all that was good. They destroyed only what was undesirable or worthless.

That's easy to do. It's easy to obey the Word of the Lord when what He asks us to destroy is utterly worthless. That's being obedient to the Lord then, isn't it? If it's worthless, we can destroy it. But if it's good, why destroy it? I mean, what kind of a God are we serving? Destroy a good sheep? All these beautiful cattle? Go ahead and destroy it. The Lord said destroy it. And obedience is better than sacrifice.

Then the Word of the Lord appeared to Samuel—again Jesus Christ came to Samuel—saying, "I regret making Saul king, for he has turned his back from following Me. He has blasphemed the Holy Spirit. I have placed My Spirit upon him. He has sung in the Spirit. He has prayed in the Spirit. But he has not performed My commandments." And Samuel was grieved and angry with Saul, and he cried unto the Lord all night in intercessory prayer for Saul.

When Samuel arose early in the morning, he was told, "Saul came to Carmel, and, behold, he set for himself a monument—a trophy of his victory—and he passed on and went down to Gilgal where he set up a heathen monument to his victory."

The victory belonged to the Lord. But Saul was taking the praise and the glory and the honor that was due the Lord and giving it to himself.

And Samuel went to Saul, and Saul said to him, "Blessed be you of the Lord. I have performed what the Lord has ordered."

But Samuel rebuked him: "What about the bleating of the sheep in my ear, the lowing of the oxen which I hear?"

Saul said, *"They* have brought them from the Amalekites."

"They." Saul acted as if he had nothing to do with *their* disobedience. *"They* brought them from the Amalekites. *The people* spared the best of the sheep and the oxen to sacrifice to the Lord *your* God, Samuel—not to the Lord *our* God, because we know we have transgressed against the Word of the Lord *our* God. We are disobedient. So we're going to bring this sacrifice to the Lord *your* God."

Then Samuel said to Saul, "Stop! Stop! I will tell you what the Lord said to me tonight."

Saul said to him, "Say on."

Samuel said, "When you were small in your own sight, were you not made the head of the tribes of Israel, and the Lord anointed you prince over Israel? And the Lord sent you on a mission, and He said, 'Go and utterly destroy the sinners, the Amalekites, and fight against them until they are consumed.' Why then did you not obey the voice of the Lord? But you swooped down upon the plunder, and you did evil in the Lord's sight. You sold yourself for a price."

Saul said to Samuel, "Yes, I have obeyed the voice of the Lord. I have gone the way which the Lord sent me, and I have brought Agag, the king of Amalek, and I have utterly destroyed the Amalekites. But the people—I have nothing to do with this—but the people took up the spoils, the sheep and the oxen, the chief of the things to be utterly destroyed, to be sacrificed to the Lord *your* God in Gilgal."

Samuel said, "Has the Lord as great delight in burnt offerings and sacrifices as in obeying the voice of the Lord? To obey is better than sacrifice, and to listen to the voice of the Lord is better than the fat of rams. For rebellion is as the sin of witchcraft, and stubbornness is as idolatry and good-luck images. Because you have rejected the Word of the Lord, He also has rejected you from being king."

And Saul said to Samuel, "I have sinned, for I have transgressed the commandment of the Lord, and your words, because I feared the people, and I obeyed their voice."

There comes a time in your life and in my life when we're going to have to fear the Lord first, before we fear anybody else. We're going to have to hear the voice of the Lord first. We're going to have to hear His voice first, above our wives, our husbands, our churches, our pastors. I don't care whose voice it is. The voice of the Lord comes first. Rebellion is as the sin of witchcraft, and stubbornness is as idolatry.

And again the message is, The Lord says He has no delight in burnt offerings and sacrifices but in obeying the voice of the Lord. And behold, To obey is better than sacrifice. To obey is the best thing of all.

6
David

(I Samuel 16—II Samuel 24
I Kings 1-2; I Chronicles 11-29)

David is called the greatest of the kings of Israel; in fact, he's one of the most prominent figures in the history of the world. Moses walked very closely with the Lord. He spoke to him mouth to mouth and face to face, but David ranks above Moses. He is the most famous ancestor of Jesus Christ. Jesus Christ is never called the son of Abraham, or the son of Isaac, or the son of Jacob, but the son of David.

We see David as a sinner. His life was like a Yo-Yo—up and down—until the Lord worked a miracle in his life. And every day in his life was a miracle.

David's character was a strange mixture of good and evil. He was filled with noble deeds, fine aspirations, and splendid accomplishments, yet his life was stained with very gross sin.

David knew where to turn when he was in sin. He knew that there was only one place where he could receive redemption, deliverance, and salvation. And he always turned back to God. No Bible character more fully illustrates the moral range of human nature, that one can be so close to the Lord and yet, the next moment, one can be such a sinner, such a backslider.

It seems impossible to imagine that the man to whom the Holy Spirit gave the Twenty-Third Psalm could commit the sins that David committed. That the man to whom the Holy Spirit gave, "Surely, goodness and mercy shall follow me all the days of my life, and I shall dwell in the house of the Lord forever," could commit adultery and murder and rationalize the whole thing.

But the spirit of the time in which David lived has to be considered, along with the temptation connected with unlimited power. David was a king, an absolute monarch. He had unlimited power, and if he chose to do his will in disobedience to the Lord, willfully and deliberately sinning, he had the power to do it. But always as he was convicted by the Holy Spirit, he came back to the Lord.

The general trend of David's life was eminently spiritual, with the Lord, but it was not always consistent. One minute he was down and doing his own thing, and the next, he was coming back to God, to receive the forgiveness of the Lord.

In his youth, David was an athlete: And David said unto Saul, "Thy servant kept his father's sheep, and when there came a lion or a bear and took a lamb out of the flock, I went after him and smote him and delivered it out of his mouth, and when he arose against me, I caught him by his beard, and I smote him, and I slew him."

This passage is a huge picture prophecy of the coming of Jesus Christ. Change the words a little: And Jesus said, "Your servant kept His father's sheep, and when there came a lion—when the enemy came, when Satan came—and took a lamb out of the flock, I went out after him. I left the ninety-nine that were secure, and I went out after that one, and I smote the enemy. I smote the adversary." Then He delivered us out of the mouth of the enemy. "When he rose against me, I caught him by his beard, and I smote him, and I slew him" This is what Jesus did for us upon the cross.

The young David was also a fine musician, and his

reputation was such that he was sent to play before King Saul.

His poetic genius came by the Holy Spirit from the Lord. The songs that were written by him were written by the Holy Spirit. They cover every facet, every aspect of life. If you study the psalms, you will see that every one of them is a psalm of thanksgiving and praise unto the Lord. No other poetry has been so constantly used by the church throughout all the centuries as the psalms of David, because they were given by the Holy Spirit.

If you have a problem, if you're living in the wilderness, start with the 140th Psalm and just read the first verse and then go to the 141st and read the first verse and continue with the first verse from the 142nd to the 150th. By the time you reach the 150th Psalm, you will have been delivered from that which you have been in, whether it's oppression or depression. Whatever situation you were in, the Lord has delivered you, because coming out of your lips is a song of praise and thanksgiving unto the Lord. You're out of the wilderness and into the Promised Land! Praise the Lord!

David was an able general. He conducted his military campaigns with great success, because when he did go out, he made sure in his heart that he was right with the Lord. He knew that if he went out without the Lord, it was to defeat.

If you and I go out without the Lord, we will be defeated, but if we go with the Lord and know that He's with us, there is no failure, there is no defeat. Remember the key words that God gave to Joshua and that Jesus gave to us: "I will never leave you. I will not forsake you. I will not fail you." There is no failure in the Lord.

David's early life was spent on his father's farm in Bethlehem, and he was the youngest of eight sons. As a shepherd, he showed great courage in protecting the flock, which is a picture of Jesus. He was divinely chosen to succeed King Saul, and he was quietly anointed by the prophet Samuel.

When we go to Israel once a year, we see the spot where David was anointed. It's up on a little hill. There are trees growing there. Mahlon and I stood there, and we worshiped the Lord. We felt the Spirit of the Lord, as the Lord anointed King David in the very same spot and poured out His Holy Spirit upon him and set him apart and divinely ordained him for the task that was before him.

That David was anointed upon his head and the oil ran over his head and clear down to his toes was symbolic of the complete protection of the Holy Spirit, that it not only covered his garments, it covered him. He was divinely protected by the Lord.

Young David became the king's harpist. After remaining at the court for a time, he returned to the farm at Bethlehem. Next he appeared upon the scene as champion of Israel against the giant Philistine, Goliath.

And the men of Israel said, "Have ye seen this man that is come up? Surely to taunt Israel he is come up, and it shall be that the man who kills him, the king will enrich him with great riches, and will give him his daughter, and make his father's house free in Israel."

And David spoke to the men that stood by him, saying, "What shall be done to the man that kills this Philistine, and takes away this taunt from Israel?"

The Philistines were not taunting Israel. They were taunting God. They were coming against the Lord.

Realizing this was so, David asked, "Who is this uncircumcised Philistine that he should have taunted the armies of the living God?"

And the people answered him after this manner, saying, "So shall it be done to the man that kills him."

And Eliab, his older brother, heard when he spoke to the men. And Eliab's anger was kindled against David, and he said, "Why have you come down?" Was Eliab, his brother lusting for the fact that he could go out against Goliath and kill him? And then he surely would receive the daughter of King Saul, and then perhaps the line of inheritance would pass through him.

David didn't contend with his brother about it. He solely depended upon the Lord.

David went out and killed Goliath, which was victory for God's people, and the deliverance from the Philistines took place. David's heroic feat won the admiration of Jonathan, the son of Saul, but the praises the people gave to David aroused the hatred of Saul.

Saul happened to be out one day, and he heard the women of Israel singing a song, saying, "Saul has slain his thousands, but David has slain his tens of thousands." With that, Satan came into Saul's heart and his mind, and he started carrying a grudge, resentment, and hatred. In his jealousy, he wanted to kill David.

What's going to happen to you and me if we harbor a grudge, resentment, or hatred? Is it going to hurt the party we're holding it against? No, it will never hurt them in any way, but it will kill us. We'll end up having ulcers, cancer, a heart attack, high blood pressure— Jesus said that if you gossip, if you speak ill, if you hold a grudge, or a resentment against your neighbor, you're guilty of murder. He said, "You shall love thy neighbor as thyself—in all situations."

Now when my neighbor's kids used to come over and break the aerial on my car radio, I used to get real upset. When they deliberately broke my sprinkler heads, I used to get really mad. And the Lord kept letting it happen, not once a week, but every day— every day until I learned to praise Him in spite of the circumstances. Finally, I released the car to Him, and the entire sprinkler system and said, "Lord, the car is Yours, the house is Yours—and the sprinkler system. If they want to break it, let them break it. If You can't protect the sprinkler system, You can't protect me."

You know, there hasn't been one head broken on that sprinkler system since. I didn't have to tell those kids a thing. But as long as I was resisting the Lord, and as long as I was getting mad and holding a grudge and resentment, they were constantly being broken.

If we release whatever grudge we have, whatever resentment we have, the hatred we have of our fellow-man, we're going to be free, and the blessings that are due us from the Lord will come to us, because He's promised us everything on the cross. He took the chastisement necessary for us to obtain our peace. Let us take the peace. It's as simple as that.

In the third part of David's life, he was a fugitive, because Saul was out to kill him. Pursued by the deadly hatred of King Saul, David was forced to lead the life of an outlaw. But there were some bright spots—

Jonathan's magnificent intercession with Saul secured David temporary restoration to the king's favor. And the generosity of David in twice sparing his enemy's life was truly remarkable.

When Saul was out to kill him, David's words over and over again were, "I will not touch the anointed of the Lord. Samuel anointed Saul king over Israel. I will not touch him. God, it's not my problem. You chose two men. You anointed me king of Israel and king of Judah, and now it's up to You to do what You have to do. I will never kill this man. I will not harm him in any way. He's out to kill me, but I'm going to turn the other cheek. Whatever is done, Lord, You will have to do it."

David was telling the Lord, "I will stand and see Your salvation. I will stand and see Your Jesus. It's up to You, Lord. I will never return evil for evil. I'll return good for evil."

In his obedience in this situation, David was truly being a man after God's own heart.

The fourth part of David's life is as king after the death of Saul. Because he was of the tribe of Judah, and the lion of Judah was coming from him, the Lord promised him a kingdom which would last forever, and a king who would be an everlasting king. He gave him this promise, and at the same time, He gave him a promise of judgment: "Because you have lived by the sword, because you have killed this Uriah, the Hittite, know that the sword will never depart from your family." He promised him that the Messiah, the Christ, would be coming from him, but then the sword would be in his family throughout his lifetime.

After David became king, all the tribes of Israel came to David unto Hebron and spoke, saying, "Behold, we are thy bone and thy flesh. In time past, when Saul was king over us, it was you who did lead out and bring in Israel, and the Lord said unto thee, 'You shall feed my people Israel. You shall be the shepherd of Israel.'"

So all the elders of Israel came to the king, to Hebron, and King David made a covenant with them in Hebron before the Lord. And they anointed David king over Israel.

David was thirty years old, and he reigned forty years as king over all Judah and over all Israel. He began his reign at the same age as Jesus began His ministry.

A notable event of David's later years had to do with the ark of the covenant: And David again gathered together all the chosen men of Israel, thirty thousand men. And David arose and went with all the people that were with him from Baale of Judah to bring up from there the ark of God, whereupon is called the name of the Lord of hosts that sitteth upon the cherubims.

And they set the ark of God upon a new cart.

Was this a phenomen of obedience? How was the ark of the covenant to be handled? It was never to be placed upon a cart of any sort. There were poles to go through the golden rings, and it was to be carried upon the shoulders of the priests, that the Word of the Lord and His everlasting covenant would be carried upon our shoulders, next to our heart, implanted in our minds.

So they placed the ark of God upon a new cart, and they brought it out of the house of Abinadab that was in the hill, and Uzzah and Ahio, the sons of Abinadab, drove the new cart. Ahio went before the ark. And David and all the house of Israel played before the Lord on all manner of instruments made of cypress wood, harps, psalteries, timbrels, cornets, and with cymbals.

And when they came to the threshingfloor of Nachon, the oxen stumbled. The ark started to fall off, and Uzzah put forth his hand to the ark of God and took hold of it.

So the anger of the Lord, righteous indignation, was kindled against Uzzah. And God smote him there for his error, and Uzzah died by the ark of the covenant.

Now, the Lord was not being a God of vengeance at this point. He did not kill Uzzah for the fact that he placed forth his hand to stop the ark of the covenant from falling. The lesson is that unholiness cannot touch the holy.

There is only one way we become holy, and that is through Jesus Christ. We are unholy; we are unclean. We are unrighteous until we come to the Lord Jesus Christ.

As a minister of the Gospel, traveling all over the country, I found a strange phenomenon, that is, I found that I was trying to help the Lord Jesus. I was trying to defend Him.

And when the Lord placed me in the hospital for thirty-three days with a heart attack, and He ministered to me every day, He said, "You are not My defense. I am your defense. I don't need your help. You need My help." That was the lesson I had to learn. We never have to defend the Word of the Lord. We never have to defend Jesus Christ. He is our defense. The living Word of God is the living Word of God. All you need to say is, "This is the Word of God. I believe it." You don't argue about it.

And David was angry with the Lord. Uzzah was one of his best servants, one of his best men. David was displeased because the Lord had broken forth upon Uzzah, and that place was called Perezuzzah (the breaking forth upon Uzzah) until this day. And David was afraid of the Lord that day. And he said, "How shall the ark of the Lord come unto me?" So David would not remove the ark of the Lord unto him into the city of David, but David carried it aside into the house of Obededom the Gitite.

Because Obededom the Gitite was a man obedient unto the Lord, with the ark of the covenant in his house, he worshiped the Lord the whole time. And as he worshiped and praised God, he was richly blessed.

And the ark of the Lord remained in the house of Obededom the Gitite three months, and the Lord blessed Obededom and all of his house.

And it was told King David, saying, "The Lord hath blessed the house of Obededom, and all that pertain unto him because of the ark of God." And David went and brought up the ark of God from the house of Obededom into the city of David with joy.

And it was so, that when they bore the ark of the Lord—they were obedient this time, bearing the ark of the Lord on the shoulders of the priests—after they had gone six paces, David sacrificed an ox and a fatling. And David danced before the Lord with all his might; he was dancing in the Spirit as the ark of the Lord was coming into Jerusalem. The Spirit of the Lord was heavy upon him. David had on a linen ephod, which means he was dressed as a priest, not as the king of Israel.

So David and all the house of Israel brought up the ark of the Lord with shouting, and with praise, and with the sound of the horn. And it was so as the ark of the Lord came into the city of David that Michal, the daughter of Saul, looked out of the window and saw King David leaping and dancing before the Lord, and she despised him in her heart.

"What kind of a king are you? Here you expose yourself before all of Israel! What Hebrew king dances in the Spirit! You're singing in a strange language, and you're dancing in a strange way. What kind of a king are you?"

And they brought in the ark of the Lord, and they set it in its place in the midst of the tent that David had pitched for it, and David offered burnt offerings and peace offerings before the Lord. As he brought in the burnt offering, he received the visible manifestation of God's acceptance of the people of Israel, and the forgiveness of all their sin, because the heavenly Holy Spirit came down and consumed the burnt offerings. And David knew that all of Israel was forgiven.

Then he brought in a peace offering, saying, "Lord, I accept Your forgiveness. I bring You this peace offering because You have now made peace with me, and I will walk out of here rejoicing and praising You from this day forward, and so will all the people of Israel."

And when David had made an end of offering the burnt offerings and the peace offerings, he blessed the people in the name of the Lord of hosts. He gave them a benediction. And he dealt among the people, even among the whole multitude of Israel, both to men and women, to everyone a cake of bread, a cake made in the pan, and a sweet cake. And all the people departed, everyone to his house.

This cake was given with a portion of wine, unleavened bread and wine. It was a picture of the communion of Jesus Christ. They partook of the unleavened bread as the covenant of the Lord came into Jerusalem.

("Bread" could be translated from the Hebrew in two ways, as bread or flesh—meat. Bethlehem in Hebrew is "house of bread." In Arabic, Bethlehem is "house of meat." It's very easy to mistranslate the word. David gave them unleavened bread and wine, but then he gave them a sweet cake, which is a cake made with raisins.)

In bringing the ark to Jerusalem, David was again being a man after God's own heart, worshiping Him. But afterward, he plunged into sin.

Bathsheba knew the king took a stroll upon his balcony at night. Is it possible that her shade was deliberately drawn back as she took her bath, or was it by mere accident? In any event, David was outside one night, and he saw her taking a bath. He was filled with the spirit of lust, and commanded Bathsheba to be brought into his court. She didn't put up a fight or argument against the king. She surrendered herself willingly—and became pregnant. Uriah, Bathsheba's husband, was away at war. David's sin would be found out. What could David do?

Then Uriah the Hittite came home on furlough, no longer Hittite. He had accepted the Lord as his personal redeemer, as his living God.

At first, David thought he had a solution. He would send Uriah home to be with his wife, and then it would be thought the child who would be born was his child. "You've fought hard in battle," David said to him. "Now you're home on furlough. Go home, take a bath, and spend some time with your wife." But Uriah was so faithful to his king and to his God that he chose to sleep on the doorstep of the king's house. He did not go home. David was still stuck with the pregnancy of Bathsheba.

David rationalized the whole thing, then: "After all, I have been commanded by God to kill all the Hittites, the Amorites, and the Jebusites," he said. And he called in Joab, his nephew who was commander-in-chief of his armies, and he said to him, "Put Uriah out in front in the hottest battle—get him killed."

Three years later, after Israel had suffered drought, famine, and pestilence because of David's sin, Nathan, the prophet of the Lord, confronted him. "You are the man that has brought all this misery upon Israel."

And David turned in repentance to the Lord and said, "Have mercy upon me, O God, according to Your steadfast love. According to the multitude of Your tender mercies and loving kindnesses, blot out my transgressions. Wash me thoroughly and repeatedly for my iniquity and my guilt, and cleanse me and make me whole and pure from my sin. For I am conscious of my transgressions, and I acknowledge them. My sin is ever before me. Against You and You only have I sinned, and done that which is evil in Your sight, so that You, Lord, are justified in Your sentence, and You are faultless in Your judgment. Behold, I was brought forth in a state of iniquity. My mother was sinful who conceived me, and I, too, am sinful.

"Create in me a clean heart, O God, and renew a right spirit within me. Cast me not away from Your presence, and take not Your Holy Spirit from within me."

David had seen what happened to Saul when God removed His Holy Spirit from him.

David had turned in complete repentance to the Lord.

Praise the Lord!

7

Solomon

(Kings 1-11)

Solomon, King of Israel, the man of wisdom and of folly, was the son of David and Bathsheba. After the death of their firstborn, David comforted Bathsheba, his wife, and went to her and lay with her, and she bore a son, and she called his name Solomon, and the Lord loved the child. And He sent a message by the hand of Nathan the prophet, and Nathan called the boy's special name Jedidiah, meaning in the Hebrew, "beloved of the Lord," because the Lord loved the child.

Solomon was both fortunate and unfortunate in his home surroundings and his parents. He was fortunate in having a father like David who was a great genius. He was fortunate that his father was enimently a man of the Lord, a man after God's own heart, that David always knew where to turn in times of trouble and distress, that David knew God as the source of all life, and that as he sinned, he always repented and came back to the Lord. But Solomon was unfortunate in that there were some elements in his father's example that would inevitably have a very bad effect upon him.

Solomon was reared in a home where polygamy was practiced, and therefore there was much jealousy and strife. David was married to quite a few women. There was also jealousy and strife among the brothers.

"Who's going to be the next king? Who's going to be the next leader? Who's going to inherit this? Who's going to receive that?"

Now, David, having many sons, had promised that Solomon should be his successor.

Bathsheba, speaking to King David, said unto him, "My Lord, you swore by the Lord your God to your handmaid, saying, 'Assuredly Solomon, your son, shall reign after me and sit upon my throne.'" She reminded him that he had taken an oath in the name of the Lord that Solomon would be the next king of Israel. And she reminded him, not that she was his wife, but his handmaid. Her humility toward David was to insure that Solomon would be the next king of Israel.

But it was not through her efforts that he would be the king. The Lord had already chosen him. But Bathsheba thought she had to help the Lord accomplish His purpose.

One of the phenomena of obedience and disobedience is that we always seem to think we have to step in and give Jesus a hand—we think He can't do it all, that we have to do it. Whenever we step in to help Him, we get into trouble. He's our defense. He's the One who helps us out. He's the source of our life.

Bathsheba went on to say, "And now, behold, Adonijah is reigning, and my lord, the king, you don't even know it. You've gotten to be an old man, and Adonijah is now reigning in your absence, and you don't even know that he's doing it. He has sacrificed oxen, fatlings in abundance, for a feast. He has invited all the king's sons; Abiathar, the priest; Joab, the commander of the army; but he did not invite Solomon, your servant. He's his half-brother. Solomon, who is not fit to be king, he's not even fit to be called a son, but he is your servant, lord king of all Israel and all of Judah." So Bathsheba humbled Solomon before the eyes of David.

What was she doing? She was playing it very cool.

"And now, my lord, O king, the eyes of all Israel are

on you to tell who shall sit on the throne of my lord, the king, after you. Otherwise, when my lord, the king, shall sleep with his fathers, I and my son Solomon shall be counted as offenders." She wanted to secure the kingship for her son before David died. She wanted to make sure he received the inheritance. She didn't know that the Lord had already chosen him.

While she was still talking with the king, Nathan the prophet came in. When he came before the king, he bowed himself before him with his face to the ground. And Nathan said, "My lord, the king, have you said, 'Adonijah shall reign after me, and he shall sit on my throne'? He has gone this day, and has sacrificed oxen, fatlings, and sheep in abundance, and has invited all the king's sons, the captains of the host, and Abiathar, the priest, and they eat and drink before him and say, 'Long live King Adonijah!' "

Was it accident, or divine appointment, that sent the prophet of the Lord in at the right time, at the right place, when the conversation was taking place concerning the next king of Israel?

Nathan went on to say, "But me, your servant, and Zadok the priest, and Benaiah, the son of Jehoiada, and your servant Solomon, he has not invited. He has not invited the prophets of the Lord, the true priests of God. Is this done by my lord, the king, that you have not shown your servants who shall succeed my lord, the king?"

Then King David answered and said, "Call Bathsheba," and she came back into the king's presence and stood before him. And the king took an oath and said, "As the Lord lives who has redeemed my soul out of all distress, even as I swore to you by the Lord God of Israel, saying, 'Assuredly, Solomon, your son, shall reign after me, and he shall sit upon my throne in my stead,' even so will I certainly do this day."

Bathsheba bowed with her face to the ground and to the king and said, "Let my lord, King David, live forever."

But King David said, "Call Zadok the priest, Nathan

the prophet, and Benaiah the son of Jehoiada," and they came before the king. And the king told them, "Take the servants of your lord, and cause Solomon my son to ride on my own mule and to bring him down to Gihon. And let Zadok the priest and Nathan the prophet anoint him there king over all Israel. Then blow the trumpet and say, 'Long live King Solomon!'"

The prophet of the Lord did anoint Solomon the next king of Israel. The true high priest of God did lay hands upon him, and he became the next king of Israel. The Lord had already prepared it in advance.

Benaiah said, "As the Lord hath been with my lord, the king, even so may He be with Solomon and make his throne greater than the throne of my lord, king David." So Zadok the priest, Nathan the prophet, Benaiah the son of Jehoiada, and the king's bodyguard, went down and caused Solomon to ride upon King David's mule and brought him to Gihon. And Zadok the priest took a horn of oil out of the tent and anointed Solomon. They blew the trumpet and all the people said, "Long live King Solomon."

Considering the age in which Solomon lived, he began his reign very well.

Early in his reign, he had a vision at Gibeon in which the Lord appeared to him and told him to ask what he would have. Solomon was a very humble man to start with, and he said, "Lord, all I want is Your wisdom and Your knowledge to rule Your people, Your inheritance, Israel."

And the Lord said, "Because you have asked wisely, I will give you the gift of the Holy Spirit, two gifts of which are wisdom and knowledge, but then I will do something else for you. I will also give you wealth. I will give you honor. I will make you the most powerful kingdom the face of the earth has ever seen." And Solomon became the wealthiest man on the face of the earth.

Solomon had asked for an understanding heart.

"Heart" in Hebrew means the will, the mind, the intellect, and the emotions.

In other words, Solomon was saying, "Give me a will that understands. Give me an intellect that understands. Give me an emotion that understands, that when I see other people, I will have such feeling for them that I can love them in spite of themselves. Make me able to love all in my kingdom in Your name, loving my neighbor as myself as king of Israel."

Because Solomon had chosen wisely, he was promised by the Lord that he should be the wisest of men and have great riches and honor. This promise was fulfilled; Solomon excelled in wisdom. He spoke three thousand proverbs, his songs numbered a thousand and five, he wrote three of the books of the Bible, and his fame spread abroad over all the earth.

But the very gifts that God gave him soon provided a doorway for the enemy, and he came in like a flood. Before long, the enemy convinced Solomon that his ally was not the Lord, but that he needed to go down into Egypt to make an alliance with Pharaoh.

But the Lord had said to Israel, "I have delivered you out of bondage. You are never to go back to Egypt. You are never to make an alliance with them." Nevertheless, Solomon went down into Egypt, and he married Pharaoh's daughter to cement the alliance. This was the first of his foreign alliances, all of which contributed to his moral downfall.

When his new wife came up from Egypt, she brought her little idol with her. And when Solomon built the temple to the Lord, he had a very beautiful temple in which to worship the Lord. But she said, " I don't expect you to take my idol and put it into the house of *your* Lord, but just build me a little shack where I can worship my idol. You worship your God, and I'll worship my god."

A few months later, she said, "Solomon, so how come your God has a great big beautiful temple, and my god has just a little shack? Would it hurt very much if we put my idol in the house of your Lord? Then we could worship together, sweetheart."

Soon, her little idol was right next to the ark of the covenant in the sanctuary of the Lord, and they were bowing down together, worshiping the living God and heathen idols.

As Solomon got hung up with one woman after another—seven hundred wives and three hundred concubines—you can guess the idolatry that entered into the house of the Lord. They all brought in their heathen abominations.

We have to fight continuously in Jesus Christ the triune forces of evil. We have to die to ourselves daily, subdue the flesh. We have to fight the enemy, Satan himself. And then we have to fight the world. Jesus says we can be in the world but not be part of it. If we remain in Him, we can remain separate from the world. We can be identified as Christians—all who look upon us can tell us by the smile we have on our faces, the way we act, the way we talk. We may never ever be able to pick up a Bible and preach the Gospel to anybody else. But they read us. We may be the only Bible they will ever read.

If we have professed to be Christians, we had better start to act and to live as Christians, and to look at the other person through the eyes of Jesus Christ, and to love them in spite of themselves the way Jesus loves us—in spite of ourselves.

Women, idolatry—and Solomon was being attacked in another area of his life at the same. His ego. People were coming in and telling him, "Solomon, there is no one as wise as you in all the face of the earth. You're the greatest of all the kings. You're the wisest of all the kings." His ego was getting inflated, bigger, fatter, and he was finally thinking he was the only person in the entire universe.

I can identify with Solomon, because the same thing happened to me, and the Lord had to humble me. He put me in the hospital for thirty-three days. I learned that if I didn't humble myself before the Lord—that's the easy way—He'd do it for me—that's the hard way.

In the fifth part of Solomon's life, he carried out the plans of his father, David. He consolidated the kingdom and engaged in many commercial ventures while his wealth and his renown grew at a fast pace. His greatest enterprise was the erection of the temple in Jerusalem. It took seven years to build the temple, which was elaborately fitted and adorned.

At the completion of the work, Solomon offered a dedicatory prayer in which he acknowledged, "There is no other God like Thee," and asked God to hear their prayers and forgive their sins.

In the sixth part of his life, Solomon was honored by a very great visit from Queen Sheba. When she went back, she was carrying a child by Solomon. So today, Haile Selassie has on his flag the lion of Judah. He truly is descended from Sheba and Solomon.

Now as Solomon increased in wealth and honor, his love of display grew upon him. He strutted around like a peacock. The wisdom and knowledge that the Lord gave him was under attack, and he permitted himself to stay under that attack.

What is it that you and I have that Solomon did not have? Jesus. We have the authority of the believer to stand up and rebuke the enemy and say, "Get thee behind me, Satan. I refuse to accept this, in the name of Jesus Christ." The enemy will flee from us when we do this. He does not have a leg to stand on. When we rebuke him in the name of Jesus of Nazareth, he has to run. When we claim the shed blood of Jesus Christ, he will flee from us, because the Lord did it all for us on the cross of Calvary. He took from us our sins, our transgressions, and our iniquities. Jesus took, upon the cross, the chastisement necessary for you to obtain your peace. He gave us peace, love, joy—all we need to do is lift up our hands and take it.

Solomon didn't have our authority over the enemy.

So, he walked around like a strutting peacock. He maintained a luxurious and extravagant establishment beyond what the resources of his people would warrant. All this eventually led to social discontent and paved the way for the disruption of the kingdom.

Solomon didn't turn back to the Lord like his father, David, did. He never realized that the Lord was the supply of his life, of his spirit, and of his soul. He remained in the attack. He ended up morally defeated, in idolatry. At the last, he plunged into sensuality, influenced by his many wives who introduced the worship of false gods into Jerusalem, not only in the sanctuary, but among all the people in Jerusalem.

Finally he was sharply rebuked, not by a prophet, but by the Lord Himself for his apostasy. The destruction of the kingdom in his son's time was foretold.

And the Lord was angry with Solomon, because his heart was turned from the Lord God of Israel, who had appeared to him twice.

If you had seen the Lord face to face and had spoken to Him and He had spoken to you, could you turn away to an idol? Could you turn and worship something that your hands had created? Could you turn and worship a TV set? Could you worship a golf course?

The Lord is a jealous God. He has a right to be righteously indignant. The Lord said, "I am righteously indignant with you, Solomon. I am holding you responsible for all this idolatry among My people. You have been the shepherd. I have given you much. To whom I have given much, of him I require much. But you didn't give Me a thing. Only lip service. You never gave Me heart service."

Solomon's life furnishes a great warning to you and me. He is known as the wisest man, yet his wisdom did not teach him self-control. He had no control upon his emotions. What he saw, he took. He wanted to do his own thing at all times. He did not permit the wisdom of God to teach him self-control. He taught well, but he failed to practice his own precepts. He preached beautifully, but he failed to listen to the sermon himself. He never heard the message that he taught. Although he was sharply rebuked by God for his apostasy, Solomon did not listen to the Lord. He did not come back to salvation. The Lord gave him one more chance to return, to repent of his evil ways, but what did he do?

Of his actual end, nothing positive is known. Whether he finally repented and returned to God has been warmly debated by students of history for years. Did he truly repent before the Lord before he died, or did he remain in his apostasy?

I would say that he never repented before the Lord. The Lord, being omniscient, being omnipresent, knowing the beginning, the middle, the end, the future, told Solomon, "Because you have turned from the Lord the God of Israel who has appeared to you twice, and I have commanded you concerning this thing that you should not go after other gods, but you did not do what the Lord your God has commanded, therefore, because you are doing this, you have not kept My covenant and My statutes which I have commanded you, I will take this kingdom. I will now tear it from you, and I will give it to your servant." The Lord was speaking about a future event, knowing that Solomon would never repent before the Lord.

And the Lord said, "However, in your days I will not do it, for David, your father's sake, but I will tear it out of the hands of your son, that even as I give it to your servant and to your son, I will send your servant, Jeroboam, back to Egypt where you took your first wife, whose statue was first brought into the house of the Lord. I will send him down there, and I will train him in being a leader, in being a general, and he will become king over Israel, as the ten tribes will have a civil war against the two tribes, and go up to Samaria and establish a kingdom there."

Jeroboam and all eighteen kings after him were each one successively worse than the other. Not one of them would ever do a thing that was right in the eyes of the

Lord. Every one of them would worship idols. Every one would be worse than his predecessor.

In the days of the Old Testament, there was only one denomination. The people were either for the Lord or they were against Him. They were either the people of God—believers—or they were heathen—unbelievers. If they didn't like the preacher, and they didn't like the sermon, they couldn't go out and become a Baptist, or a Methodist, or a Presbyterian. What did they do? They killed the prophet of the Lord and said, "We don't want to hear the message."

Isaiah was sawed in half. Zechariah was taken into the house of the Lord in front of the sanctuary of the Lord and killed right there. And the Lord, even in the New Testament, spoke to the people of Israel, calling them, "those who have shed the blood of the prophets." There was blood upon Jerusalem, and Jesus said, "I'm not weeping for Myself, but I'm weeping for you."

In His last moments upon the cross, He said, "Father, forgive them, for they know not what they do." He was still being taunted as He went as the lamb of God which takes away the sin of all the world. He was taunted by the people of Israel: "If You are the Messiah, if You are the big shot Savior, if You are the son of David, go ahead and save Yourself."

And they said, "Let His blood be upon us and upon all our generations to come."

But praise God for Jesus Christ who took that stigma out of our hands and said, "Father, forgive them." He granted us forgiveness right then and there as He shed His blood for us while we were still in our sin. God gave Solomon every possible gift, but Solomon did not use them for the glory of God. Instead, he permitted the enemy to come in and attack him in the very same gifts that God gave him. And there were all the abominations in the house of the Lord. Again God says, "Obedience is better than sacrifice."

The Lord will speak to us continually about being obedient. He personally appeared to Solomon and said, "You have not been obedient. Exactly what I told you not to do, you did. I'm giving you another chance to repent." Did Solomon open his mouth and say, "I repent, Lord"? No. He didn't say a word. He stayed in his own sin. He accepted what God gave him in judgment, and he never interceded and said, "Lord, take Your judgment from me." His father, David, had turned to the Lord, even with the sin of Bathsheba, and had pleaded with the Lord, "Create in me a clean heart. Renew a right spirit within me, and please, Lord, take not Your Holy Spirit from me."

David had seen what happened to Saul. As the Lord removed His Holy Spirit from Saul, he was open to the attack of the enemy. An evil spirit came into him, and the end of Saul was that of a totally unsaved man, a maniac. He was insane.

Saul wanted to speak to the Lord one more time, but he had already passed from grace into judgment. So he went to the witch at Endor and asked her to bring up the spirit of Samuel, because Samuel was already dead. But a witch can't bring up the spirit of a prophet, or anyone else. She brought up a counterfeit from the enemy, from Satan's camp, and that counterfeit told him, "Where I am today is where you are going to be tomorrow. In hell."

The next day, Saul was wounded in battle. He asked his guard, his armed bodyguard, to kill him, but he refused. Then Saul fell on his own sword and killed himself.

In the ninth chapter of Genesis are the first commandments God gave. One of them is, "If you shed your own blood, I will require it of you." That's a prohibition against suicide. So where did Saul go? He was without salvation. Where did Solomon go? He was without salvation.

But David, his father, was saved because he constantly went back to the Lord. He constantly acknowledged his sin. He constantly acknowledged his weakness. He constantly said, "Lord, I need Your help. I can't do it without You."

And this is you and I. We can't do it without Jesus Christ. We're weak. We revert back to our flesh, and we must remember that Jesus is with us always, standing next to us, never leaving us, never forsaking us, never failing us. There is no failure in the Lord, and there is power in the name of Jesus if we call upon His name.

I have been to hospitals where the only word that a paralyzed person or an unconscious person could utter was Jesus, and by saying the name of Jesus, they have been delivered, healed, saved—just by saying the name Jesus. It is the most powerful name on earth, in the heavens, in the universe. Say it.

JESUS!

8
Elijah
(I Kings 17 — II Kings 2)

Nothing is known of the parentage of Elijah, the prophet of fire. He was one of the most unique and dramatic characters of biblical history. Rugged in appearance and dress, he was a prototype of John the Baptist. His whole life was a thrilling pictorial scene of contemporary events—and a prophecy of what would take place in the future.

In Elijah's unheralded appearance before the idolatrous king of Israel, Ahab, he announced a prolonged drought: Elijah the Tishbite, of the temporary residence of Gilead, said to Ahab, "As the Lord God of Israel lives, before whom I stand, there shall not be dew nor rain these years, but according to the word of the Lord. The Lord has spoken it, and it shall be done. There shall be a drought in the land of Israel, because you have sinned. You and your wife, Jezebel, are about the worst pair that God has ever seen. Every king after you will be just as bad as you, but you two are really a pair."

After Elijah delivered the prophecy, God sent him into the wilderness: The word of the Lord came to him, saying, "Go from here and turn east and hide yourself by the brook Cherith that is east of the Jordan. You shall drink of the brook, and I, the Lord your God, have commanded the ravens to feed you there." A raven is a scavenger, and therefore, it's an unclean bird, an un-kosher bird. God said, "I have commanded a scavenger to feed you. You are now going to eat from that which is unclean, and it is by the command of the Lord." So he did according to the word of the Lord. He went, and he dwelt by the brook Cherith that is east of the Jordan, and the ravens brought him bread and flesh in the morning, and bread and flesh in the evening, and he drank of the brook.

What kind of flesh were the ravens bringing Elijah? It wasn't kosher flesh, it was not clean flesh. But Elijah had the divine promise of the Lord, divine guidance, that he was to eat what the ravens brought him. In the phenomenon of obedience unto the Lord, he was sustained by those unclean birds.

The Lord, you know, has a very good sense of humor. When you get tied up in your own self-righteousness, He gets you out of it. He did the same thing with Peter when He showed him the vision of the sheet coming down. He said, "Peter, kill and eat."

Peter said, "I never ate un-kosher food in my whole life, Lord, so how do You expect me to eat un-kosher food now?"

And the Lord said, "Kill and eat." He showed him the vision three times. Then He sent him to the house of a Gentile, a heathen.

There, Peter broke the law automatically, the minute he ate with the Gentiles, as far as the 613 rabbinical laws were concerned.

And then God had the nerve to baptize the Gentiles in the Holy Spirit! Peter went one step further, and baptized them in water. Then Peter went back to Jerusalem and told them all about it, and they all got upset.

"How dare you, and how dare God take heathens and baptize them in the Holy Spirit? Didn't you know this is reserved for us Jews only?"

Do we have Christians like that today, who say that the gift has been reserved for us only, and let's not

99

give it to anybody else? We've become legalistic, haven't we?

Elijah had told the king that there was going to be a drought in the land, that there'd be no rain. And every source of water was dried up. Elijah was in the same predicament as everybody else, because judgment, love, grace, and mercy fall upon the righteous and the unrighteous at the same time.

Elijah was being obedient to the Lord, and yet his water was dried up because there was no rain in the land. His obedience and his faith were being tested. Did he say, "What am I going to do now, Lord? You got me into this situation. Where am I going to get water from?" Was he going to do like the people of Israel have done for thousands of years, yell and scream and murmur to the Lord? (The word "murmur" in Hebrew doesn't mean to whisper, because when a Jew murmurs, he yells.) No.

The minute the water was dried up, the Word of the Lord came to him. Jesus Christ Himself, the *Logos* Himself, appeared to Elijah. And He said, "Arise— what are you sitting there for? Go to Zarephath, which belongs to Zidon, and dwell there; and behold, I have commanded a widow there to provide for you."

So Elijah arose and went to Zarephath. When he came to the gate of the famine-stricken city, behold, a widow was there gathering sticks. He called to her and said, "Bring me a little water in a vessel that I may drink." She had just enough for herself. As she was going to get it, he called to her and said, "Bring me a morsel of bread in your hand." And she said, "As the Lord your God lives—" not "as the Lord *my* God lives, but "as the Lord *your* God lives," because she was not a believer, but she knew a prophet of the Lord when she saw one.

She could tell a prophet of the Lord like people can tell a Christian—by the smile on his face. We are known as the people of a smile. People can see the love, the bubbling over of the love of Jesus Christ, coming through our lives.

The widow recognized Elijah as a prophet of the Lord, and she said, "As the Lord your God lives, I have not a loaf baked, but only a handful of meal in the jar and a little oil in the bottle. I'm gathering two sticks that I may go in and bake it for me and my son that we may eat and not die."

In the Hebrew, it says, "and *not* die." In the English, it says, "die." The widow was not about to die, because the Lord already had His phenomenon of obedience in action.

God had sent Elijah the prophet to be fed of her. How could she die if she was going to feed him?

Elijah said to her, "Fear not. Go and do as you have said, but make me a little cake of it first and bring it here to me, and afterward prepare for yourself and your son. For thus saith the Lord, the God of Israel, 'The jar of meal shall not waste away, or the bottle of oil fail, until the day the Lord sends rain on the earth.'"

The Lord was giving her a promise that He would supply all of her needs from this point on, despite the famine, despite the drought, despite whatever was in the land. He would take care of her.

After these things, the son of the woman, the mistress of the house, became sick, and the sickness was so severe there was no breath left in him. The strain of the famine has been too great for him. And he lay dead before the prophet. And she said to Elijah, "What have you against me, O man of God? Have you come to me to call my sin to remembrance and to claim my son? Did you come here to convict me of my sins?" Remember, she was not a believer. "I fed you when I had only enough food for me and my son. Now what is it that you have against me that you came here to put me under condemnation?"

And he said to her, "Give me your son," and he took him from her bosom and carried him up into the chamber where he stayed, and he laid him upon his own bed. And Elijah now cried unto the Lord and said, "O Lord my God, have You brought further calamity upon this widow with whom I sojourn by slaying her son?

It is enough of a calamity that she is a widow. You have given them a promise of food. You have promised to supply all of their needs, and now the boy is dead. What is it that You've done, Lord?" Elijah was not afraid to speak to the Lord. The Lord had spoken to him.

The Lord wants us to be specific when we pray. He wants us to tell Him exactly what we want. He knows what our needs are, but when we specify them to Him, He builds up our faith. If we need a healing, let's say exactly what we need. If we have an illness, and we don't know what it is, then we tell the Lord, "Lord, You know what this illness is, and now we take authority over it in the name of Jesus, and we commit it to You, and we bind it to You in the name of Jesus Christ." Then it is done.

After Elijah had prayed, he stretched himself upon the child three times. Why three times? Is it possible that he was thinking about the Father, the Son, and the Holy Spirit?

And he cried to the Lord and said, "O Lord my God, I pray You, let this child's soul come back unto him." And the Lord heard the voice of Elijah, and the soul of the child came into him again, and he revived. There was a resurrection right there in the Old Testament. And Elijah took the child and brought him down out of the chamber into the lower part of the house and gave him to his mother, and Elijah said, "See, your son is alive." And the woman said to Elijah, "By this I know that you are a man of God, and that the word of the Lord in your mouth is truth." She was making an affirmation of faith. By this miracle, she became a believer in the Lord.

Every time the Lord performs a miracle—a small healing, a big healing—it's part and parcel of the resurrection of Jesus Christ. We have touched the resurrection, and by this, others will know that He lives. Others will come to believe. The Lord performs miracles to bring others to Himself.

And it came to pass after many days, that the Word of the Lord came to Elijah and said, "Go, show thyself to Ahab, and I will send rain upon the earth."

And when Ahab saw Elijah, Ahab said to him, "Are you the guy who is troubling all of Israel?"

Elijah replied, "I have not troubled Israel, but you have. The Lord says you are the one who has troubled Israel, and your father's house has troubled Israel by forsaking the commandments of the Lord and following Baalim. Therefore send and gather to me all Israel at Mount Carmel, and the four hundred and fifty prophets of Baal, and the four hundred prophets of the asherah who eat at Queen Jezebel's table."

So there were four hundred and fifty prophets of Baal and four hundred prophets of those who worshipped the male sex organ, eight hundred and fifty false prophets.

So Ahab sent unto all the Israelites and assembled the prophets at Mount Carmel. Elijah came there to all the people and said, "How long will you halt and limp between two opinions? How long will you stand and follow a path that is neither right nor wrong, but yet you rationalize it by saying, 'We are worshiping God in the right, and we are worshiping the Baal and the asherah in the wrong. If we worship God in the morning, and we worship the idols in the afternoon, isn't that all right?'" And he said, "How long will you falter between two opinions?"

Later on in the New Testament, Jesus said, "I spit you out of My mouth, because you're neither hot or cold. You can't make up your mind." And He made another statement, saying, "If you're not for Me, you're against Me."

Elijah told them, "If the Lord is God, follow Him. But if Baal is god, then follow him," and the people did not answer him a word. After all the thousands of years that they had seen miracle after miracle of the Lord God of Israel, the true living God, they didn't even answer one word.

Then the prophet Elijah challenged the prophets of Baal to a fiery test:

"Now let two bulls be given to us. Let them choose one bull for themselves, cut it in pieces, lay it on the wood, but put no fire to it. I will dress the other bull. I will lay it on the wood, and I will put no fire to it. Then you call on the name of your god, and I will call on the name of the living Lord. The one who answers by fire, by the Holy Spirit, let Him be known as the true living God."

And all the people opened up their mouths and said, "It is well spoken. Now we're going to put God to the test. The one who answers, we'll acknowledge Him as the Lord. Let's see His miraculous power one more time, then we'll believe."

So the prophets of Baal took the bull that was given to them. They dressed it and laid it on the wood, and called on the name of Baal from morning until noon saying, "O Baal, hear and answer us." But there was no voice. No one answered. And they leaped upon the altar that they had made.

And at noon, Elijah mocked them, saying, "Cry aloud, for he is a god. Either he is musing, or he's gone aside, or he's on a journey, or perhaps he's asleep. Maybe he's out on a date. He's got to be awakened." And they cried aloud and cut themselves after their custom with knives and lancets. They cut their bodies. And the blood gushed out upon them. Midday passed, and they played the part of prophets until time for the offering of the evening sacrifice. There was no voice. There was no answer. No one paid attention. They were worshiping a god they had made with their own hands. The false prophets had failed completely.

Then Elijah said to all the people, "Come near unto me." Why did he ask the people to come near unto him? The Lord said, "You draw nigh unto Me, and I will draw nigh unto you." Elijah wanted all of Israel to see the miracle that was about to take place. He had the faith to believe that the minute he called upon the living God, the minute he opened his mouth and asked the Lord to send down the fire of the Holy Spirit, the Lord would do it. He had the faith and the obedience to believe.

And Elijah said to all the people, "Come near unto me," and the people came near him, and he repaired the old altar of the Lord that had been broken down by Jezebel. She had broken it down so the people couldn't bring their burnt offerings unto the Lord. Elijah took twelve stones, according to the number of the tribes of the sons of Israel. And with the stones, Elijah built an altar in the name and the self-revelation of the Lord.

He made a trench about the altar as great as would contain two measures of seed. He put the wood in order; he cut the bullock in pieces; he laid it on the wood, and said, "Fill four jars with water and pour it on the burnt offering and on the wood. If we're going to put God to the test, let's soak it real good." And he said, "Do it the second time," and they did it the second time. And he said, "Do it the third time," and they did it the third time." He did it the first time in the name of the Father, he did it the second time in the name of the Son, he did it the third time in the name of the Holy Spirit.

The water ran round about the altar; and he filled the trench also with water. Then, at the time of the offering of the evening sacrifice, Elijah the prophet came near, and said, "O Lord, the God of Abraham, Isaac, and Israel, let it be known this day that You are God in Israel, and that I am Your servant, and that I have done all these things at Your word in perfect obedience. Hear me, O Lord. Hear me that these people, these stiff-necked arrogant people, may know You, that You are the Lord their God, and that they have taken their hearts away from idolatry, and that they have turned their hearts back to You, O Lord."

And the minute he said that, the fire of the Holy Spirit—the fire of the Lord—fell, and it consumed the burnt sacrifice. It consumed the wood. It consumed the stones. It consumed the dust and licked up the water that was in the trench. Everything was taken up. The Lord consumed everything. He said, "I am a devouring fire, and nothing will stand in the way of the Holy Spirit."

And when the people saw the fire, they fell on their faces, and they said, "The Lord, He is God; the Lord, He is God."

And Elijah said, "Seize the prophets of Baal; let not one of them escape." They seized them, and Elijah brought them down to the brook Kishon, as God's law required, and slew them there.

And Elijah said to Ahab, "Go up and eat and drink, for there is the sound of abundance of rain." So Ahab went up to eat and to drink. And Elijah went up to the top of Carmel. He bowed himself down upon the earth, and he put his face between his knees. And he said to his servant, "Go up now and look toward the sea."

And he went up and he looked and he said, "There is nothing."

And Elijah said, "Go again seven times."

By His Holy Spirit, God gave Elijah discernment that there would be rain if he prayed. If he stood still in perfect obedience and in faith, the rain would come. All he had to do was to be obedient unto the Lord and send up his intercessory prayer.

At the seventh time, the servant said, "A cloud as small as a man's hand is arising out of the sea."

And Elijah said, "Go up and say to Ahab, 'Get your chariot and go down, lest the rain stop you.'" In a little while, the heavens were black with windswept clouds, and there was a great rain. And Ahab went to Jezreel. And the hand of the Lord was on Elijah.

In the Hebrew, the "hand of the Lord" being upon a prophet means that the Lord is pushing him, guiding him, doing exactly as He wants to do with the prophet. Elijah could not go anywhere except where the hand of the Lord guided him or pushed him.

So Elijah girded up his loins, and he ran before Ahab to the entrance of Jezreel, nearly twenty miles. Could he have run it in twenty miles in a downpour of rain, except the hand of the Lord was upon him?

And Ahab told Jezebel all that Elijah had done, and how he had slain all the prophets of Baal with the sword. Then Jezebel sent a messenger to Elijah, saying, "So let the gods do to me, and more also, if I do not make your life as the life of one of them by this time tomorrow. You slew my prophets of Baal, so now I'm going to kill you." She cursed him. She pronounced a death sentence upon him.

What happened? Did Elijah stand by faith and obedience and say, "Praise the Lord that she's out to kill me"? No. He was afraid. He had just called down the fire of the heavenly Spirit. He had called down the rain of God. The Lord had used him to raise the son of the widow from the dead. But he was afraid of Jezebel.

Elijah arose and went for his life, and he came to Beersheba over Judah, which is eighty miles out of Jezreel's realm, and he left his servant there, but he himself went a day's journey into the wilderness, and he came and sat down under a long broom or a juniper tree. Then he asked the Lord that he might die. He said, "It is enough now, Lord. Take away my life. I'm no better than my fathers. I don't want to live anymore."

As he lay asleep under the broom tree, behold, an angel touched him and said to him, "Get up. Arise and eat. You're not going to lie here starving to death, because I'm going to take care of you." He looked, and behold, there was a cake baked on the coals and a bottle of water at his head, and he ate and he drank and he lay down again.

Then the Angel of the Lord, the Redeeming Angel Himself, Jesus Christ, came the second time and touched him and said, "Arise and eat, because the journey is too great for you. You can't do it by yourself, but with Me, you can."

So he arose and he ate, and he drank, and he went in the strength of the food forty days and forty nights to Horeb, the mountain of God. (Horeb is the area; the mount is called Mount Horeb; and the top of the mount is called Mount Sinai where the Lord gave the ten living words, the Ten Commandments.)

And there he came to a cave. He lodged in it, and behold, the Word of the Lord came to him. Jesus came to him and said, "What are you doing here, Elijah? What are you hiding for? I told you to arise."

He replied to the Lord, "I have been very jealous for the Lord God of hosts. (I've been jealous for You, Lord, because I'm Your defense, Lord. You really cannot defend Yourself, but I have been Your defense.) I've been very jealous for You, Lord, because the Israelites have forsaken Your covenant. They have thrown down Your altars. They have killed Your prophets with the sword, and I—only I—am left, and they seek my life to take it away."

And the Lord said, "Go out and stand on the mount before the Lord." And, behold, the Lord passed by, and a great strong wind rent the mountains, and broke in pieces the rocks before the Lord; but the Lord was not in the wind. And after the wind was an earthquake, but the Lord was not in the earthquake. And after the earthquake, a fire, but the Lord was not in the fire. And after the fire, a sound of a gentle stillness and a still small voice.

And when Elijah heard the voice, he wrapped his face in his mantle, and he went out and stood in the entrance of the cave, and behold there came a voice to him again and said, "What are you doing here, Elijah?"

He said again, "I have been very jealous for the Lord God of hosts because the Israelites have forsaken Your covenant. They have thrown down Your altars. They have slain Your prophets with the sword; and I—only I—am left; and they seek my life, to destroy it."

And the Lord said unto him, "Go, return on your way to the wilderness of Damascus. And when you arrive, anoint Hazael to be king over Syria. He will become an enemy, but I want you to anoint him. I want you to be obedient unto Me. And anoint Jehu, son of Nimshi, to be king over Israel, and anoint Elisha, son of Shaphat of Abelmeholah, to be prophet in your place. And him who escapes from the sword of Hazael, Jehu shall slay, and him who escapes the sword of Jehu, Elisha shall slay."

The Lord was going to bring judgment, love, grace, and mercy in the same time and in the same place. There was going to be a heathen king anointed by a prophet of the Lord to bring judgment upon Israel. There was going to be a king of Israel anointed to bring back the judgment of the Lord upon the enemy. And there was going to be a prophet anointed in place of Elijah. The Lord had a plan in mind. He was going to take Elijah up, to translate him into heaven.

So Elijah left there and found Elisha, son of Shaphat, whose plowing was being done with twelve yoke of oxen, and he drove the twelfth. Elijah crossed over to him and cast his mantle upon him. Elisha left the oxen, and he ran after Elijah and said, "Let me kiss my father and my mother, and then I will follow you."

And Elijah, testing Elisha, said, "Go on back. What have I done for you? You settle it for yourself." So Elisha went back from him, and he took a yoke of oxen, and he slew them, boiled their flesh with the oxen's yoke as fuel, and he gave to the people and they ate. Then he arose and he followed Elijah and he served him.

Then the Word of the Lord came to Elijah the Tishbite, saying, "Arise, get up. I want you to go into the court where they're out to kill you. Go in there, meet King Ahab, king of Israel and Samaria. He is in the vineyard of Naboth, which he has gone to possess. Say to him, 'Thus saith the Lord, "Have you killed and also taken possession?" Thus saith the Lord, "In the place where the dogs licked the blood of Naboth, shall the dogs lick your blood, even yours."'"

And Ahab said to Elijah, "Have you found me, O my enemy? The troubler of Israel, have you found me?"

And he answered, "I have found you because you have sold yourself to do evil in the sight of the Lord.

You sold yourself to Satan, and now the Lord has found you. He's the one who is bringing judgment upon you. 'Lo,' says the Lord, 'I will bring evil on you and utterly sweep away and cut off from Ahab every male, bond and free. You will never have anything from this point on. I will make your household like that of Jeroboam, the son of Nebat, and like the house of Baasha, son of Ahijah, for the provocation with which you have provoked Me to anger and made Israel to sin.'"

Also the Lord said of Jezebel, "The dogs shall eat Jezebel by the wall of Jezreel. With all her idolatry, with her worship of the male sex organ, this abomination that she brought into Israel, the dogs shall eat Jezebel by the walls of Jezreel.

"Him of Ahab who dies in the city, the dogs shall eat, and him who dies in the field, the birds of the air shall eat, for there was none like unto Ahab who sold himself to the enemy to do evil in the sight of the Lord, incited by his wife Jezebel." Jezebel was the power behind the throne. Ahab did very abominably in going after idols, as did the Amorites whom the Lord cast out before the Israelites.

When Ahab heard the words of Elijah, he tore his clothes, put sackcloth on his flesh, and fasted and lay in sackcloth and went quietly. And the Word of the Lord came to Elijah the Tishbite saying, "Do you see how Ahab humbles himself before Me? Because he humbles himself before Me, I will not bring the evil in his lifetime; but in his son's day, I will bring the evil upon his house." The Lord accepted repentance from Ahab.

Moab rebelled against Israel after the death of Ahab. And King Ahaziah fell down through a lattice in his upper chamber in Samaria and was sick. And he sent messengers, saying, "Go ask Baalzebub, the god of the Philistines of Ekron, if I shall recover from this illness."

But the Angel of the Lord Jesus Christ again appeared to Elijah the Tishbite and said, "Arise, go up and meet the messengers of the king in Samaria and say to them, 'Is it because there is no God in Israel that you're going to inquire of Satan, Baalzebub the god of Ekron?' Therefore the Lord said, 'You Ahaziah shall not leave the bed on which you lie, but you shall surely die.'" Then Elijah departed.

On Elijah's last journey, accompanied by Elisha, he traveled through the country until they reached the Jordan River where Elijah smote the waters with his mantle, and the two passed over on dry ground. As they stood conversing together, Elisha made his farewell request of Elijah. He said, "I want a double portion of that Holy Spirit which is upon you."

And Elijah told him, "If you see me taken up, you will know you have received it. If you don't see me taken up, know that you have not."

Suddenly a chariot of fire separated the two friends, Elijah and Elisha, and Elijah was taken up by a whirlwind in the chariot into heaven. Elisha saw him go.

On the Mount of Transfiguration, in the New Testament, Elijah reappeared with Moses and talked with Jesus Christ. Jesus Christ was already king, but the prophecy stated in the Old Testament that He was to be king, prophet, and priest. Moses passed on the Melchizedek priesthood to Jesus Christ, and Elijah passed on the mantle of the prophet to Jesus Christ, and He became King, Prophet, and Priest, the One who would be *perfectly* obedient.

9
Elisha
(II Kings 2-13)

There is a very striking resemblance between the life of Elijah and that of Elisha. Not only do their names sound alike, but the main events of their lives run in much the same channels. They are twin figures in Hebrew history. The Lord had given Elijah a disciple, one who could carry on his ministry in the exact manner that the Lord had prescribed for Elijah.

After Elisha had seen Elijah taken up by a whirlwind into heaven, he took the mantle that fell from Elijah and struck the waters and said, "Where is the Lord God of Elijah?" And when he had struck the waters, they parted this way and that, and Elisha went over. He had received a double portion of the Holy Spirit of God.

Elijah had brought waters of refreshment in times of drought, and Elisha would do the same thing.

During a prolonged drought, the king of Israel went with the king of Judah and the king of Edom, and they made a circuit of seven-days' journey, but there was no water for the army nor for the animals following them. Then the king of Israel said, "Alas, the Lord has called us three kings together to be delivered into Moab's hand."

But Jehoshaphat said, "Is there no prophet of the Lord hereabout, whom we may inquire of the Lord? That we may have intercessory prayer go up? Let's ask of the Lord, and we know the Lord will deliver Jehoshaphat, king of Judah."

One of the king of Israel's servants answered, "Elisha, son of Shaphat, who served Elijah, is here."

Jehoshaphat said, "The Word of the Lord is with him. (Jesus is with him. In the beginning was the Word and the Word was with God and the Word was God.) And if the Word of the Lord is with him, all he needs to do is command, and it shall be done by His perfect will."

So Jehoram, king of Israel, and Jehoshaphat and the king of Edom went down to Elisha, and Elisha said to the king of Israel, "What have I to do with you? Go to the prophets of your wicked father, Ahab, and your wicked mother, Jezebel."

But the king of Israel said to him, "No, for the Lord has called us three kings together to be delivered into the hand of Moab."

And Elisha said, "As the Lord of hosts lives, before whom I stand, surely were it not that I respect the presence of Jehoshaphat, king of Judah, I would neither look at you nor see you, King Jehoram. But now bring me a minstrel." And while the minstrel played a song of praise and thanksgiving to the Lord, the power of the Lord came upon Elisha. The power of the Lord was the *dunamis,* the dynamite. The Holy Spirit descended in that double portion that he asked for upon Elisha.

And he said, "Thus saith the Lord, 'Make this dry brook bed full of trenches.' For thus saith the Lord, 'You shall not see wind, or rain, yet the ravine shall be covered with water, so that you, your cattle, and your beasts of burden may drink.'"

Elisha went on to say, "This is just a light thing in the sight of the Lord, a small miracle for the Lord to fill up a bunch of trenches without wind, without rain.

You just dig, and the Lord will supply the water. And He will deliver the Moabites into your hand.

"You shall smite every fenced city, every choice city. You shall fell every good tree. You shall stop up all wells of water and mar every good piece of land with stones."

In the morning, when the sacrifice was offered, behold there came water by the way of Edom, and the country was filled with water. The miracle had taken place.

Elijah had gone to a widow who was in sore distress because of the famine in the land. By the Holy Spirit, he had provided all her needs and even raised her son from the dead. Elisha, who had asked for a double portion of the Spirit, was approached by another widow.

Now the wife of a son of the prophets cried to Elisha, "Your servant, my husband, is dead, and you know that your servant feared the Lord, but the creditor has come to take my two sons to be his slaves."

(The creditor was disobeying the commandment in the book of Leviticus which stated that if somebody came to you for a loan, and you had enough to lend him the money, you shouldn't lend it, but you should give it to him. The Lord would replace it for you in more than a double blessing. The Lord was the one who had entrusted you with this financial abundance in the first place.)

Elisha said to the widow, "What shall I do for you? Tell me, have you for sale anything of value in the house?"

She said, "Your handmaid has nothing in the house except a jar of oil. That's the only material possession I have in the entire world, just one jar of oil."

Then he said, "Go around and borrow vessels of all your neighbors, empty vessels, and not just a few. Get as many as you can. And when you come in, shut the door upon you and your sons. Then pour out the oil that you have into all those vessels, setting aside each one when it is full."

So she went from him and shut the door upon herself and her sons who brought to her the vessels as she poured the oil. When the vessels were all full, she said to her son, "Bring me another vessel, and he said to her, "There's not one left." Then the oil stopped multiplying.

Then she came and told the man of God, and he said, "Go sell the oil, pay your debt, and you and your sons live on the rest." The Lord supplied every one of her needs. She didn't have to lose her sons to the creditor. She paid her debts with the oil the Lord had multiplied. It was a miracle.

Elijah had raised the son of a widow from the dead. Elisha would do the same thing.

One day a child went out with his father with the reapers. But he said to his father, "My head, my head." His head was hurting him. The man said to his servant, "Carry him to his mother." And when he was brought to his mother, he sat on her knees till noon and he died. And she went up and laid him on the bed of the man of God, Elisha, and shut the door upon him and went out. And she called to her husband and said, "Send me one of the servants and one of the donkeys that I may go quickly to the man of God and come again."

She knew where to go. She had to run and find the man of God to intercede for her with the Lord. But our Intercessor is Jesus Christ who is constantly interceding for us. He gave us an accomplished healing and accomplished deliverance, and accomplished salvation on the cross of Calvary that we can enter the throne of grace boldly and in confidence.

The woman's husband didn't understand. He said, "Why go to him today? It's neither new moon nor sabbath."

And she said, "Don't worry, honey; it'll be all right." She didn't tell him the boy was dead. Then she saddled the donkey and said to her servant, "Ride fast. Do not slacken your pace for me unless I tell you." So she set out and came to the man of God at Mount Carmel.

When the man of God saw her afar off, he said to Gehazi, his servant, "Behold, yonder is that Shunammite woman. Run to meet her and say, 'Is it well with you? How is your peace? How is your shalom? Is everything well with you? Well with your husband? Is it well with the child?'"

And she answered, "It is well."

When she came to the mountain to the man of God, she clung to his feet. Gehazi came to thrust her away, but the man of God said, "Let her alone, for her soul is bitter and vexed within her, and the Lord has hid it from me, and He has not told me."

Then she said, "I desired a son of my Lord. Did I not say unto you, 'Do not deceive me'?" That she had borne a son in the first place was a miracle. "Did I not tell you, Elisha, 'Do not deceive me? If the Lord gives me a son, he's going to be a son to live to the honor, and praise, and glory of the Lord.' And now he's dead."

Then he said to Gehazi, "Gird up your loins, take my staff in your hand, and go and lay my staff on the face of the child. If you meet any man, do not salute him. Do not greet him. If he salutes you, if he greets you, if he says, 'Hello,' 'Good morning,' if he says anything, do not answer him."

The mother of the child said, "As the Lord lives, and as my soul lives, I will not leave you." And he arose and followed her.

Gehazi passed on before them and laid the staff on the child's face, but the boy neither spoke nor heard. So he went back to meet Elisha and said to him, "The child has not awakened. He's still dead."

When Elisha arrived in the house, the child was dead and laid upon his bed. So he went in, shut the door upon the two of them, and prayed to the Lord. He went up and lay on the child, put his mouth on his mouth, his eyes on his eyes, and his hands on his hands. And he stretched himself on him and embraced him, and the child's flesh became warm. Then he returned and walked in the house to and fro and went up again and stretched upon him seven times, and the child sneezed seven times. Then the child opened his eyes.

Then Elisha called Gehazi and said, "Call the Shunammite." So he called her, and when she came, he said, "Take up your son." She came and fell at his feet, bowing herself to the ground, then took up her son and went out. Again, the resurrection of the dead.

Both Elijah and Elisha performed miracles for persons outside the boundaries of Israel. Elijah had multiplied the food supply of the woman at Zarephath, and she had come to know God. Elisha would be God's agent to heal a Syrian and bring him to a knowledge of the living Lord.

A Syrian was even more of a heathen than the woman at Zarephath because the Syrians from that day till this day are still attacking Israel. Naaman, who was the commander of the army of the king of Syria, was a great man with his master. He was accepted and acceptable because by him the Lord had given victory to Syria. He gave victory to Syria over the people of Israel because of the heart of Naaman. He had already touched that heart. He had already touched that person. Even Naaman didn't know it, but he would come to know the Lord and to love the Lord, because he was already touched by the Lord. All he needed to do was to open up his mouth and make his profession and believe with his heart.

The victory was given to Syria because Naaman was a mighty man of valor—a man who cannot be bought for any price—but he was also a leper.

The Syrians had gone out in bands and brought away a captive out of the land of Israel, a little maid, and she waited on Naaman's wife. She said to her mistress, "Would that my lord were with the prophet who is in Samaria, for he would heal him of his leprosy."

Naaman went in and told his king, "Thus and thus said the maid from Israel."

And the king of Syria said, "Go now, and I will send a letter to the king of Israel," and he departed and took

117

with him ten changes of raiment. And he brought the letter to the king of Israel. It said, "When this letter comes to you, I will with it have sent my servant Naaman that you may cure him of leprosy."

When the king of Israel read the letter, he rent his clothes in a state of mourning, and he said, "Am I God to kill and make alive that this man sends to me to heal a man of leprosy? What does he think I am? Am I the Lord? Can I heal him of leprosy? I can't even heal a cut finger. What is he trying to do now, put me in a trap? I'm in enough trouble with the king of Syria. Now is he trying to trap me so he can destroy my kingdom entirely?"

When Elisha, the man of God, heard that the king of Israel had rent his clothes, torn his garments, and was in a state of mourning, he sent to the king asking, "Why have you rent your clothes? Let Naaman now come to me, and he shall know that there is a prophet in Israel. There's somebody in Israel who can reach the Lord, and the Lord being gracious, merciful, loving, He will even heal a leper who is a non-believer, and He will cause him to believe by the miracle that will take place."

Naaman came with his horses and chariot, and he stopped at Elisha's door. Elisha sent a messenger to him, saying, "Go and wash in the Jordan seven times, and your flesh shall be restored, and you shall be clean."

Naaman knew the waters of Syria very well. They were nice and clean, but the muddy Jordan? He was not about to go down and wash in the Jordan River.

Naaman was angry, and he went away saying, "Behold I thought surely he would come out and stand and call on the name of the Lord his God and wave his hand over the place and heal the leper. This is my idea of how a miracle should take place. This is how I want it done."

Don't you and I tell the Lord the very same thing? But He's not always going to work it the way we want it, is He?

Naaman said, "Are not the Abana and Pharpar, rivers of Damascus, better than all the waters of Israel? May I not wash in them and be cleaned?" He turned and went away in a rage. And his servant came near to him and said, "My father, if the prophet had bid you to do some great thing, would you not have done it? How much rather then, when he said to thee, 'Wash and be clean'?"

Then he went down and dipped himself seven times in Jordan, and his flesh was restored like that of a little child, and he was clean.

A miracle like this took place two years ago when I took a group to the Holy Land. The secretary of the pastor of a church in San Jose was born with allergies. Her entire body was covered with scabs and itching, and she had been taking medication all her life. As I stood in San Jose, preaching this message, the Lord said that if Sandy would go on the trip and be baptized in the Jordan, He would heal her of all the scabs, the allergies, itching—everything. But she would have to go believing and trusting the Lord that as soon as she was baptized in the Jordan, she would be healed.

I gave her the message of the Lord, and she said, "Well, Norman and I can't go, because we just came back from our vacation, and his boss would not give him any more time off."

I said, "Well, this was the Lord's message, and if it was the Lord's message, the Lord has prepared the way. So just have Norman ask his boss tomorrow if he can have the time off." And he went in and asked his boss, and he didn't even finish asking before the boss said, "You can have the time off."

And we arrived at the Jordan River and baptized Sandy in the Jordan, and that day—three years ago— she gave me her pills, all her medication. I have them with me as a living witness and testimony. She hasn't taken another pill, and she's completely healed. The phenomenon of obedience, being obedient unto the Lord.

Naaman returned to the man of God, he and all his company, and stood before him and said, "Behold, now I know that there is no God in all the earth but in Israel, that He is the true living God. So now accept a gift from your servant."

And Elisha said, "As the Lord lives before whom I stand, I will accept none." He urged him to take it, but Elisha refused.

Naaman then said, "I pray you, let there be given to me, your servant, two mules' burden of the earth of Israel." He wanted some of the earth of Israel because he realized what he was going to get back into when he got back to Syria. (In that day, it was thought that each land had its own God, and that God could be worshiped only on the soil of the land to which He belonged.)

"For your servant will henceforth, from this day forth, offer neither burnt offering, nor any sacrifice to any other god but only to the true living Lord, the God of Abraham, Isaac, and Jacob. He has healed me. He has cured my leprosy, and I know the living God. In this thing, the Lord pardon your servant, that when my master, the king, goes into the house of his god Rimmon to worship there, and he leans on my hand, and I bow myself in the house of Rimmon, the Lord pardon your servant in this thing."

Naaman was saying, "I want you to intercede for me between me and the Lord. I have to go serve my king. This is my job, but I will never offer any sacrifice to any other god except to the true God. But I must go into the house of Rimmon, who is a heathen god, which is idolatry, and the king will lean on my hand, and I'll have to bow down with him. Now you ask the Lord to forgive me before this thing is done."

And Elisha told him, "Go in peace. The Lord knows your heart. The Lord is full of love, grace, and mercy. Go in peace. He knows you have to do it, to serve your king, that your heart is really worshiping the true God." So Naaman departed from him a little way.

Elijah had pronounced the judgment of the Lord upon Ahab and Jezebel. Elisha performed a similar task.

Elisha came to Damascus, and Benhadad, the king, was sick, and he was told, "The man of God has come here."

So the king said to Hazael, "Take a present in your hand, and go and meet the man of God and inquire of the Lord by him, saying, 'Shall I recover of my disease? Ask of the Lord.' I have no other alternative. I have gone to all the houses of idolatry. I have petitioned all the gods that I made with my hands, and none of them seem to answer me. So now, go inquire of the Lord. Go inquire of the prophet of the Lord. Perhaps we'll get an answer."

So Hazael went to meet Elisha, and he took a present with him of every good thing in Damascus, forty camels' loads, and stood before him and said, "Your son, Benhadad, who happens to be king of Syria, has sent me to you asking, 'Shall I recover from this disease?'"

And Elisha said, "Go and say unto him, 'You shall certainly recover,' but the Lord has shown me that he certainly will die."

Why does it seem that Elisha is in an act of deception here? He's a prophet of the Lord.

Elisha stared steadily at Hazael until he was embarrassed, and the man of God wept before the Lord.

And Hazael said, "Why do you weep, my lord?"

He said, "Because the Lord has already shown me the evil that will come upon Israel from you and from the country of Syria. You will burn their strongholds. You will slay their young men with the sword. You will dash their infants in pieces, and you will rip up their pregnant women."

And Hazael said, "What is your servant, a dog, that he should do this monstrous thing? Why would I do such a thing?"

And Elisha answered and said, "The Lord has shown me that you will be king over Syria after Benhadad dies."

Then Hazael departed from Elisha and came to his master, who said to him, "What did Elisha say unto you?" And he answered, "He told me you would surely recover." But the next day, Hazael took the bedspread and dipped it in water and spread it on the Syrian king's face so that he died, and Hazael reigned in his stead.

There was no deception. Elisha, by the Spirit of the Lord, the double anointing of the Holy Spirit that was upon him, saw the murder that was about to take place. Hazael murdered his king, he smothered him, because if he hadn't killed him, he would have recovered from the disease. Elisha gave Hazael the right message. He told him to tell the king that he would recover from the disease, but he knew from the Spirit of the Lord that the king was going to die by the hand of man. Hazael would become king of Syria, and he would go in and do exactly as the Lord said he would do. He would take and burn. He would slay the young men with a sword. He would take the infants, dash them in pieces, and he would rip up the pregnant women. Cruelty beyond what we could think or dream.

At one time the king had sent to Elijah a captain of fifty men with his fifty to seize him. He found Elijah sitting on a hilltop and said, "Man of God, the king says, 'Come down.'"

Elijah said to the captain of fifty, "If I am a man of God, then let fire come down from heaven and consume you and your fifty." And fire fell from heaven and consumed him and his fifty men. Elijah, the prophet of the Lord, had called down the vengeance of the Lord upon the unbeliever. And there was a parallel to this in the life of Elisha.

As Elisha went up from Jericho to Bethel one day, some maturing and accountable boys—they were at least seventeen years old—came out of the city and mocked him and said to him, "Go up in a whirlwind, you baldheaded, dirty old man. Go up, you dirty, baldheaded man." And Elisha turned around and looked at them and called a curse down on them in the name of the Lord. And two she-bears came out of the woods and ripped up forty-two of the boys. And Elisha went from there to Mount Carmel and from there he returned to Samaria.

Why did he call down a curse upon them? Because they mocked him? Or were they mocking the Lord? Elisha had just healed the waters of the spring at Jericho through the power of the Holy Spirit. The boys actually came against the power of the Holy Spirit. And Elisha was righteously indignant as they came against the miracle they had seen. They were mocking the power of the Lord. So he called down the vengeance of the Lord upon them, and the Lord sent out these she-bears to destroy forty-two of the boys.

In spite of the similarities between the miracles performed by the two prophets, Elisha was not just a mere echo of Elijah, his fiery predecessor. There was a marked difference between the temperaments of the two men and their general attitude toward society and mankind. Elijah was a solitary figure like John the Baptist. His life was largely spent in an unavailing struggle with the evils of his times, and he had periods of great depression. He didn't have a double portion of the Holy Spirit; he only had a single portion, and he would occasionally revert back to his flesh. He would go hide, and he would say, "Lord, I want to die. They have killed all your prophets. Nobody's left except me, and I'm feeling sorry for myself."

Elisha's temperament was entirely different. He had received the gift of a double portion of God's Holy Spirit, and this enabled him to lead a triumphant life as he mingled with his fellowman. We have no record that he ever complained of his lot. In whatever circumstance he found himself, he constantly praised the Lord. He never fled from his enemies, and he never lost his courage. He stood on the promise that was given back in the days of Joshua: "Have I not commanded thee, 'Be strong and of good courage, for I will never leave thee, I will never forsake thee, and I will never fail thee'?" He stood upon that promise of the Lord. Even upon his deathbed, he seemed to be full of power.

Power seemed to remain in him even after his death: And Elisha died, and they buried him. And bands of Moabites invaded the land in the spring of the next year. As a man was being buried on an open bier, such a band was seen coming, and the man was cast into Elisha's grave. And when the man being let down touched the bones of Elisha, he revived and stood on his feet.

This was the very same resurrection power, the very same Holy Spirit, that raised Jesus from the dead.

Elisha performed more miracles than anybody else in the Old Testament with the exception of Moses, because he asked for a double portion of the Holy Spirit, and he did receive it.

Hazael, as prophesied by Elisha, oppressed Israel all the days of Jehoahaz. But the Lord was gracious to them, had compassion on them, and returned to them —not because of their obedience to God, but because of the Lord's obedience to Himself. When He makes a promise, He keeps a promise. As He makes a covenant, He keeps His covenant.

So Hazael, king of Syria, died, and Benhadad, his son, reigned in his stead, and Jehoash, son of Jehoahaz, recovered from Benhadad, son of Hazael, the cities which he had taken from Jehoahaz, his father, by war. And three times Jehoash recovered the cities of Israel. The miraculous power of the Holy Spirit continued in operation as long as obedience was there.

We have to be obedient to the Lord, and if we remain obedient in the Lord, anything we ask the Lord, He will grant.

The phenomenon of obedience is the surrendering totally to the Lord our will, bringing our will to His will, taking our intellect out of the way so that we're able to hear the voice of the Lord and receive His wisdom and His knowledge. He wants us to worship Him

with all our heart, our soul, and our mind, meaning
that we are to worship Him with our will, with our intellect, and our emotion. As we remain obedient to the
Lord Jesus Christ, this is worshiping Him in spirit and
in truth. If we know that He is the way and the truth,
we know that He is the life. There's no other life except
in Jesus Christ.

Praise the Lord.

10
Jonah
(Jonah 1-4)

The book of Jonah is the most ill-used and the least understood of all the books of the Bible.

The controversy surrounding the story of the great fish—is it true? is it impossible?—has been a cause of confusion and has obscured the great spiritual truth which the book has to teach. The purpose of Jonah's adventure was to teach him, and through him, Israel and all mankind, a lesson that had to be learned.

And the lesson that had to be learned by the prophet Jonah was not merely that God accepts repentance. If that were all, chapter four of Jonah would be irrelevant and unnecessary. Nor can it be only the lesson that the Gentiles, too, meaning heathen, also are God's creatures, worthy of pardon.

Jonah's reluctance to deliver the message which was given to him by the Lord was because if he was the agent of bringing the warning to the Ninevites, he would become the agent of their salvation. That the Lord chose him, a Hebrew of the Hebrews, to go to a heathen city and preach a message of salvation was about to destroy Jonah's faith in his living God. That was the way he saw it, that God was going to destroy his faith by sending him into the camp of the enemy, the Ninevites, who were attacking Israel constantly. To even offer a message of salvation to those heathen people took a lot of nerve on God's part. Jonah couldn't understand it. So the essential teaching of the book of Jonah is that nobody, heathen or otherwise, should ever be denied God's love, God's care, and God's forgiveness. This is the entire teaching of the book.

We should not begrudge God's salvation, His love, His care, or His mercy to anybody. Jonah begrudged the fact that God was going to grant salvation to the people of Nineveh if they accepted the message and if they did repent. It is this grudging which is so superbly rebuked throughout the whole book, and most of all, in the final chapter, which must rightly be considered the climax of the story.

Jonah, the son of Amittai, was mentioned in II Kings 14:25 during the reign of Jeroboam II: Jeroboam restored Israel's border from the entrance of Hamath to the sea of Arabah, according to the word of the Lord God of Israel, which He spoke by His servant Jonah, The son of Amittai, the prophet from Gathhepher. This clearly puts Jonah in the first half of the eighth century before Christ.

Jonah got his message when the Word of the Lord came to him. (In the beginning was the Word, and the Word was with God and the Word was God.) The Word Himself, Jesus Christ, appeared to Jonah, saying, "Arise. Get yourself up from where you're sitting feeling sorry for yourself. Arise. Go to Nineveh, that great city, and proclaim against it, for their wickedness is come up before Me."

But Jonah arose to flee unto Tarshish, the furthermost point of civilization at that time, to get away from the presence of the Lord. He knew he could not escape God, that no matter where he went, the Lord would go with him, just as He had promised in Deuteronomy 31:6. But Jonah thought he could escape from hearing the voice of the Lord.

Trying to escape from the presence of the Lord, from the shekinah glory of God and the Holy Spirit of God,

Jonah went down to Joppa, and he found a ship going to Tarshish. He paid the fare thereof, and he went down into it to go with them unto Tarshish from the presence of the Lord. But the Lord wanted him in His divine will, in His perfect will, so the Lord heralded a great wind into the sea. There was a mighty tempest in the sea, so that the ship was like to be broken.

Many a modern historian has stated that this story didn't take place, that it's just an allegory, just a story put in the Bible to show us what obedience is all about. But Jesus Christ Himself verified and confirmed it. He spoke about Jonah, saying, "As Jonah was in the belly of the fish three days and three nights, so shall the son of man be."

So the Lord brought a great wind, and the ship was about to be broken, and the mariners were afraid, and they cried every man unto his own god. They were heathens, idol worshipers. Each man was crying unto his own god, and to lighten the ship, they took everything that was in the ship, and tossed it into the sea.

Where was Jonah? He was totally unconcerned, down in the innermost part of the ship fast asleep. He was escaping from the presence of the Lord, figuring if he went far enough, he wouldn't hear God's voice, and the conviction of the Holy Spirit would not come upon him.

The shipmaster came to Jonah and said, "What do you mean that you sleep? Arise. We're all calling upon our gods. You get up from the bottom of the ship, come up on top of the deck, and you call upon your God, that your God will think upon us that we perish not. Our gods are not answering us. Perhaps your God is the true God. Call upon Him, and perhaps we will not perish."

And they said, every one to his fellow, "Come, let us cast lots that we may know for whose cause this evil is upon us. So they cast lots, and the lot fell upon Jonah. And they said to him, "Tell us, we pray thee, for whose cause this evil is upon us. What is your occupation?

Where do you come from? What is your country? And of what people are you?"

And he said to them, "I am a Hebrew, and I fear the Lord, the God of heaven, who made the sea and the dry land."

Then the men were exceedingly afraid and said unto him, "What is this thing that you have done?" For the men knew, as he witnessed to them, that Jonah was fleeing from the presence of the Lord. They were afraid of the living God, of the true God, as they were in this turmoil and this hurricane. The sea was in an uproar.

Then they said unto him, "What shall we do? What shall we do unto you that the sea may be calm unto us?" For the sea grew more and more tempestuous.

He said unto them, "Take me up, cast me forth into the sea, so the sea shall be calm unto you. I'm the cause of this evil which is upon you, because I am fleeing from the presence of the Lord." They had been touched by the witness that he gave to them. Would they act as heathens now, or would they act as people who are touched by the Lord?

He said, "For I know that for my sake this great tempest is upon you." Nevertheless, the men refused to throw him in. They rowed hard to bring the ship to land, but they could not, for the sea grew more and more tempestuous against them. Wherefore, they cried unto the Lord and said (notice the power of witnessing to even a heathen), "We beseech Thee, O Lord, we beseech Thee, let us not perish for this man's life, and lay not upon us innocent blood. Don't cause us now to toss him into the sea. Cause us to do it another way." They were calling upon the living God. "For Thou, O Lord—You have done as it has pleased You, O Lord."

So they took up Jonah, and cast him forth into the sea, and the sea ceased from its raging. Then the men feared the Lord exceedingly as they saw the miracle take place instantly.

What did they do? They offered a sacrifice unto the

Lord, and they made vows. They said, "When we get to land, we're going to go and bring forth another sacrifice unto the Lord. We're going to give a pledge, a tithe, and an offering, and we're going to believe in the living God." After a short witness and a testimony, they were turned from their idolatry and came to know the living God.

In Hebrew oral tradition, we are told that on the day of creation when God created the sea monsters and the fish, He prepared a leviathan for one mission, and that was to swallow Jonah. You'll find it in the Talmud, but not in the Bible. The Lord prepared a great leviathan to swallow up Jonah, and Jonah was in the belly of the fish three days and three nights.

Then Jonah prayed unto the Lord his God out of the fish's belly. He didn't beseech the Lord, he claimed a promise, he claimed a victory before the victory could be seen. He said, "I called unto the Lord out of my affliction, and He answered me. I have already called upon Him, and He has answered me, even though at this moment I can't see the answer."

Have you and I called upon the Lord out of our affliction and we haven't seen the answer as yet? Do we faint? Do we give up hope, or what do we do? God tells us to stand and see His salvation, to be still and know that He is God.

Jonah, still in the belly of the whale, said, "I called out of my affliction unto the Lord, and He answered me. Out of the belly of hell cried I, and You heard my voice.

"For you, Lord, did cast me into the deep, in the heart of the seas, and the flood was round about me; all Your waves and all Your billows passed over me. And I said, 'I am cast from before Your very eyes, from before Your presence from which I tried to escape. Yet, I know for a certainty that I will look again toward Your Holy Temple. That surely goodness and mercy will follow me all the days of my life.'" Jonah was claiming a promise. He said, "The waters compassed me about, even to my very soul. The deep was round about me. The weeds were wrapped around my head."

How many seaweed prophets do we have? How many of us have seaweed wrapped around our necks, and we have no way out? What is the way out? Jesus Christ. Start praising Him. Start thanking Him for the seaweeds wrapped around your neck, and say to the Lord, "I have called upon the name of the Lord in my affliction, and You have heard me and You have delivered me." Claim the promise that by His stripes you are healed. It's an accomplished fact. It's already been done. All we have to do is lift up our hand, take it, receive it, appropriate it, and stand upon that promise. We may not see it today, or this afternoon, or tomorrow, but we will see it.

Jonah lived to see it.

So he said, "The weeds were wrapped around my head. I went down to the bottoms of the mountains; the earth with her bars closed upon me forever. There was no way out except You, Lord, the source of all life. I had to look up, and I did look up, and I did call upon You, Lord, and I know You heard my voice. You have brought up my life from the pit of hell, O Lord My God. When my soul fainted within me, when I had nothing left, by Your Holy Spirit, You caused me to remember You, Lord. I remembered the Lord, and my prayer came in unto You into Your Holy Temple.

"They that regard lying vanity and arrogance forsake their own mercy. They who get hooked on anything that comes between themselves and the Lord Jesus Christ forsake their own mercy."

Jonah continued praising God in the song of thanksgiving, in the song of praise, in the song of prayer, and he said, "But I will sacrifice unto Thee with the voice of thanksgiving. I'm going to thank You, Lord, for the circumstances that I find myself in. I'm going to thank You for this seaweed wrapped around my neck. I'm going to thank You, Lord, that I am down at the bottom of hell. That which I have vowed, I will pay—my pledge, my tithe, my offering. I will walk into Your holy sanctuary by Your love, and Your grace, and

Your mercy, and I will bring my offering unto You, O Lord." And he said, "Salvation is of the Lord." In the Old Testament, "salvation" is the name of Jesus in Hebrew. So he said, "Jesus is of the Lord; I have been delivered by Jesus."

And the minute he said this, finishing his song of praise and thanksgiving, the Lord spoke unto the fish, and it vomited out Jonah upon the dry land.

Then the thing from which Jonah had tried to escape, the voice of the Lord, came a second time, giving him the same word, the same commission, to go into the city of Nineveh: The Word of the Lord, Jesus Christ, came unto Jonah the second time, saying, "Arise, get up. Go to Nineveh, that great city, and make unto it the proclamation that I bid thee. Just say the words that I tell you to say. You're not the Savior, and you're not the Deliverer, I am. You just do what I tell you to do, be obedient unto Me, and I will do the rest."

How many of us have gone out and gotten frustrated because we've planted seeds for Jesus Christ and wanted to do the watering and the harvesting too? We can't. He says some of us will plant the seeds, some of us will water the seeds, and some of us will harvest the seeds. He may put us into any category.

So Jonah arose. This time he was not going to run from hearing the voice of the Lord. He knew that no matter where he went, the Holy Spirit was going to come upon him and give him the same message.

So Jonah went to Nineveh according to the Word of the Lord. Now Nineveh was an exceeding great city of three days' journey. And Jonah began to enter into the city a day's journey, and he proclaimed the message that the Lord gave him. "Yet forty days, and Nineveh shall be overthrown." This was all the Lord told him to say. "You have forty days to repent. Now if you listen, and you believe God's Word, and you do repent, the deliverance is at hand."

And the people of Nineveh believed God. Why? Their hearts were already prepared. They believed

God for His Word. So they proclaimed a fast. They put on sackcloth, from the greatest of them even to the least of them, and the tidings reached the king of Nineveh, and he arose from his throne, took off his robe from off himself and covered himself with sackcloth. He sat in ashes in a state of mourning. And he caused it to be proclaimed and published throughout all of Nineveh by the decree of the king and his nobles, saying, "Let neither man nor beast, herd nor flock, taste any thing. Let them not feed, nor drink water. But let them be covered with sackcloth, both man and beast, and cry mightily unto God; yea, let everyone of them turn from his evil way and from the violence that is in their hands. Who knows whether God will not turn and permit Himself to be entreated?" (It's an incorrect translation to say here, "if God will repent." God is not a man that He will repent.)

"See if God will permit Himself to be entreated of you, and turn away from His fierce anger that we perish not." And God saw their works. He saw their hearts. Their hearts were sincere in their repentance. And they turned from their evil ways, and the evil which God said He would do unto them, He did it not.

Nineveh was saved. Jonah had been obedient unto the Lord. But He said, "Lord, why did You have to put me through this whole thing? Why? I knew You were going to save them in the first place. I know You're a God who's longsuffering, gracious, kind, merciful. Did You have to put me through the whale, the leviathan, through the weeds wrapped around my neck? I knew that if I brought that message, You were going to save them. So now, I'm going to resent You for it, Lord. Why didn't You do it by Yourself? Why did You have to use me?"

The Scripture tells us it displeased Jonah exceedingly, and he was angry. He was angry with the Lord, and he prayed unto the Lord, and he said, "I pray thee, O Lord, was not this my saying when I was in my own country? Did I not tell You, Lord, that I knew You were going to save them? Therefore, I fled from before Thee unto Tarshish, for I knew that You are a gracious God, that You are a compassionate God, You are a longsuffering God, that You are abundant in mercy, and You would be entreated of the evil that You were about to do. Therefore, now O Lord, take, I beseech thee, my life from me, for it is better for me to die than to live." He said that all he wanted to do was die. He didn't want to live anymore. "God, You saved these heathen people. You saved these enemies of Israel. I don't want to live any longer. I want to do just like Elijah did. I'm going to go hide in a cave, and I'm going to do that which would take my life away from me."

Jonah said, "Therefore, Lord, take my life from me, because if You don't, I'm going to do it myself, for it is better for me to die than to live."

And the Lord spoke to him again. He said, "Hey Jonah, are you really greatly angry? How angry are you?"

So Jonah went out of the city, and there he made a booth, and he sat under it in the shadow so that he might see what would become of the city.

And the Lord God prepared a gourd and made it to come up over Jonah that it might be a shadow over his head to deliver him from the evil which he was about to do to himself. He was sitting out in the hot sun, and the hot east desert wind was blasting him. He would die of dehydration; he would die of the sun. So the Lord showed him His love and His grace, and His mercy. The gourd was a protection for him, to deliver Jonah from the evil which he was bringing upon himself. And Jonah was exceedingly glad because of the gourd. But during the night, God prepared a worm, and when the morning rose the next day, it smote the gourd that it withered. The worm killed the gourd.

And it came to pass, when the sun arose, that God now prepared a vehement east wind; and the sun beat upon the head of Jonah that he fainted and requested for himself that he might die, and he said, "It is better for me to die than to live."

And God said to Jonah—He spoke to him again—"Jonah, how angry are you? Are you greatly angry for the gourd? First, you were angry because I saved and delivered the people of Nineveh. Now are you angry because I destroyed the gourd?"

And Jonah answered the Lord, saying, "I am greatly angry, even unto death. I want to die. I can't deal with a God like You with all the mercy, and the love, and the grace that You show."

And the Lord said, "You have had pity on the gourd for which you have not labored, neither made you it to grow. It came up in one night, and perished in one night, and should I not have pity on Nineveh, that great city, where there are more than six score thousand persons that cannot discern between their right hand and their left hand and also much cattle?"

The people were almost as children. They couldn't tell the difference between right and wrong. The Lord had never spoken to them, had never given them the message, never given them the commandments of life, never talked to them about everlasting life in the Lord, and He said, "Yet you are grieving over a gourd which you had nothing to do with. You didn't plant the seed, you didn't water it, you didn't harvest it. Shouldn't I, the Lord your God, have pity upon all these thousands of people in the city of Nineveh? They are made in My image and in My likeness." And Jonah finally got the message, that salvation is not to be denied to any person, that God is no respecter of persons.

What does God expect you and me to do? He still gives the same message as we open any part of any book of the Bible—obedience, obedience, obedience leaps out at you from every page. God wants us to be an obedient people.

He stated, "If My people, who are called by My name, shall humble themselves, and pray, and seek My face, and turn from their wicked ways; then will I hear from heaven, I will forgive their sin, and I will heal their land."

We have water pollution; we have a smog problem. What do we need to do? We need to pray and turn from our wicked ways and repent and become truly a Christian nation, following after the Lord Jesus Christ, being living witnesses for Him. If we do that, what's His part of the bargain? He said, "Then will I hear from heaven, and I will forgive their sin and heal their land." There will be healing in our land. There is no way this nation is going to get rid of the pollution problem except by becoming truly a Christian nation dedicated to the Lord Jesus Christ.

Is there peace? Did Jesus say there would be peace? The end-time prophecies state that there will be wars, there'll be rumors of wars. It will be as it was in the days of Noah. It will be as it was in the days of Sodom and Gomorrah—abominations, homosexuality, Satan worship. All these things will take place before the end time comes. And we are living in the end time.

The Lord is telling us to expect a miracle every day of our lives as we walk in perfect obedience to Him. There's only one way to escape in the end time from that which is about to take place. And that is John 3:16. It's so simple, and yet we miss it. We should repeat it, and teach it to our children over and over again until we truly believe it. That God loved you and me enough that He gave His only begotten Son that whosoever believed in Him should not perish but have everlasting life. What then? Do we sit on our laurels and say, "Well, we're saved. We've picked up the promise of John 3:16." Is that all? Or is there something that you have to do?

The Scripture tells us in Romans 10:9 that you have to profess with your lips and believe with your heart that Jesus died for you, He was buried and rose again, and that you rise with Him again to a new life.

Jesus went to the waters of baptism. Why? To fulfill all righteousness for you and me. He had no need to be baptized because He was without sin. But He did it for us, that when we are baptized, we go into the waters of death with Him, and we rise into a new life. Without going into the waters of baptism and following in His footsteps, we will not receive the additional power we need to resist the temptation and the assault of the enemy that comes upon us.

Acts 2:38 says, "Repent, and be baptized in the name of the Lord Jesus Christ for the remission of sins, and you shall receive the gift of the Holy Spirit." Every Christian who has repented and been baptized in the name of Jesus Christ has received the gift of the Holy Ghost. This is not the Baptism in the Holy Spirit; this is the gift of the Holy Spirit.

The Baptism in the Holy Spirit brings the power of the Holy Spirit that Christ told the apostles to wait for in Jerusalem. It was the dunamis from on high, the dynamite from on high, so they could go out in power and in authority and act in His name. When He baptizes us in the Holy Spirit, He gives us this power of attorney—to go out and act in His name.

He said, "You shall do greater things than I have done. You shall lay hands on the sick, and they shall recover. Any deadly thing that you eat or drink—it shall not harm you. You shall speak with new tongues." He didn't say you "might," or "perhaps," or "The sick might recover." He said, "You shall lay hands on the sick and they shall recover." Do you believe it? If you believe it, it happens. It takes place.

How deep is your faith? How shallow is your faith? What do you believe? Do you believe every word that Christ told you is true? Do you believe that by His stripes you are healed?

I believe it. I believed it when I was dying on my deathbed when I had my heart attack. I was ready to go home with the Lord. I was just like Jonah, wanting to get out of the whole thing. But the Lord said, "I still have a ministry for you, but I'm teaching you a lesson because you had reached the point where you thought that you were indispensable, that there was nobody else in the world who could go out and be an evangelist or minister just like you could. Yes, you are a completed Jew. Yes, I have taken you, a rabbi, and I've

137

completed you in Myself, and I've given you the Baptism in the Holy Spirit, but you're not indispensable."

And for the thirty-three days that I was in the hospital, the Lord spoke to me constantly, until I was humbled before Him. And He said, "I'm going to plant it in your mind so far and so deep that obedience is better than sacrifice that never again will you reach the point that you can go out and play My part, pretending to be Jesus Christ."

He said, "I am the Lord. You have placed yourself before Me."

Many of us have the tendency to do this. We place ourselves before the Lord. For example, we come between our mate and the Lord Jesus Christ. We won't permit Him to minister to our mate. When we have problems at home, we play the part of Jesus. We're going to preach the Gospel to our mate, no matter what. We're going to show him in verse by verse Scripture that this is what Jesus said. You know what's happening? You're turning your mates off.

What does the Scripture say? It says, "By the godly example of your life, you can win your mates over to Jesus Christ." You have made a profession with your lips. You believe with your heart. Now live the profession. Be the example. Be Christlike, and pretty soon, your wife or your husband who has not come to the Lord will say, "Honey, sweetheart, you have something that I want. You have the peace that passes all understanding, and I don't understand it. What is it that you have? I want the very same thing."

Many of us have families that are not saved. The Lord gave us a promise in Acts 16:31 that if we believe in the Lord Jesus Christ, we and our families and our households will be saved.

If we claim that promise, we can claim the whole bunch for salvation. I've claimed my family for salvation. I know that I will see my family, who are all Jews, come to know and love Jesus Christ as I do. They will come to know and to love Him as their Messiah.

Praise the Lord!

11

Isaiah

(Isaiah 1-66)

Isaiah, a prophet of the Lord, was the son of Amoz. He prophesied during the reigns of Uzziah, Jotham, Ahaz, and Hezekiah.

Isaiah's name in Hebrew means "salvation is of the Lord." Every time you see the word "salvation" in your Bible, it is the name of Jesus in Hebrew. Simeon, an old high priest in Jerusalem, prayed his whole life, "Lord, before I die, let me see the salvager of Israel." As he held the baby Jesus in his arms, he said, "I praise You, Lord. I thank You that I have lived to see the salvation of the Lord—I have lived to see the Jesus of the Lord."

Isaiah is generally regarded as the greatest of the Old Testament prophets. First, because he was pre-eminently the prophet who brought forth the message by the Holy Spirit of the redemption of all of God's people through Jesus Christ. He is the missionary prophet, the one who would tell us more about Christ Jesus than any other prophet in the entire Bible. There's more of Jesus in Isaiah than there is in the New Testament, believe it or not.

Isaiah was regarded as the greatest of the Old Testament prophets in the second place because many of the passages of Scripture in the Book of Isaiah are among the finest of any literature. Many modern scholars have studied this poetical prophecy as a botanist would study a flower, and they have dissected and microscopically analyzed the message given to Isaiah by the Holy Spirit. By the use of their scientific method, the beauty and the unity of the book is almost forgotten as the different parts are pulled apart piece by piece for examination.

No matter what the scholars say, as far as the Hebrew people are concerned, from the time of Isaiah until now, there has been only one Isaiah. The enemies of God, some people and Satan himself, would like to have us believe that there was a first Isaiah, then a second Isaiah, then a third Isaiah. They say they have discovered that there were four different Isaiahs.

But I stood in Jerusalem in the building called the Shrine of the Book where they have discovered among the Dead Sea scrolls, the complete book of Isaiah. And they now state that it's not just two thousand years old. Isaiah appeared eight hundred years before Christ. So they know that it's at least twenty-eight hundred years old. And yet that Hebrew is the same Hebrew that I read in my Bible right now. It has not changed. It is one complete book.

And the Lord gave the entire message to Isaiah to bring to God's people and to the world that there was coming a Savior into the world, the hope of all the world, and the hope of Israel.

Section one of the Book of Isaiah refers chiefly to the events leading up to the captivity of Israel. It contains exhortations, the warning of God to Israel through Isaiah that divine judgment was coming upon God's people for their failure to be obedient unto Him.

We have the same message given to us today. The Lord is telling us we are in the end times, and the phenomenon of obedience, not disobedience, had better take place in our lives. We had better be prepared, and we had better look up, for our redemption draweth nigh. The Lord is on His way back. The King is coming soon.

The message that divine judgment was coming upon Israel was mingled with the prediction of better days and of the coming Messiah who would save the people of Israel. If the people would turn to Him, He would be their Savior. The Lord had already prepared an everlasting covenant to which Christ would be obedient unto death.

The second part of Isaiah is prophecy respecting the nations surrounding Israel, mainly the predominant highly civilized nations of the time—Assyria, Babylon, Moab, Egypt, the land of the Philistines, Edom, and Tyre. They were arrogant and heathen. God would use them as instruments of judgment to teach the lesson of obedience to His people. If they would not learn by the Word Himself being revealed to them, they were going to have to learn the hard way. They were going to have to get spanked, to be chastised. They would have to go into captivity, but the Lord said, "I will spare you this if you will repent and you will turn to Me and ask for forgiveness. I will forgive you. I am a just and faithful God. For thousands of years I have told you turn to Me and I would turn to you."

The way the Bible puts it is, "Draw nigh unto Me, and I will draw nigh unto you." He said, "You have to take a step of faith. You have to come to Me, and if you come to Me, I'll meet you halfway." Then He said, "Come, let us sit down, My children. Maybe I've been too good a Father to you. Maybe I've spoiled you rotten. Let's talk about it. Let's reason it out together, and let's see what we come up with. Let's communicate one with another."

The third part of the Book of Isaiah concerns the sins and the misery of the people of Israel. At the time Isaiah was written, there was not one intercessor found in all of Israel to intercede with God asking him to change His judgment. The message was brought to the people of Israel. Nobody could say they did not hear the Word of God. But nobody took the time, the trouble, the effort to say, "Lord, I am now standing in intercessory prayer, and I am entreating You to lift this judgment from us."

Esther called out all of the Jews during the time of Haman when he was about to destroy all of the Jews, and they fasted for three days. And they repented before the Lord, and the judgment was lifted, because they repented before God. He said, "I am just and faithful to forgive you of all your sins if you come to Me and ask for forgiveness."

In the Book of Isaiah, God said to the people of Israel, "You have come to My house, you have brought Me gifts, you have brought Me sacrifices, thinking that you were going to bribe Me, but I will not be bribed. You have brought Me lip service, and I detest it, I abhor it, I reject it. All I want from you is your obedience, your love, and the proper attitude of your heart, the circumcision of your heart. That's all I ever asked of you from the day I brought you out of bondage in Egypt. I want your obedience—obedience is better than sacrifice. Obedience is all I want from you."

A song of confidence in God emerges in chapter 26 and 27 in God's care over His vineyard. He calls Israel His vineyard. She must blossom and bring forth fruit. He chose Israel as a people to be missionaries, as their father Abraham was a missionary. God said, "I sent him in the entire land of Caanan to bring a message of salvation, of deliverance, and of healing to the heathen people, and this is what I want you to do. I want you to go out into all the world and bring the message, the Gospel of the Old Testament, that I shall be your God and you shall be My people. That I will make you holy because I am holy, that I have called unto Myself a nation of a kingdom of priests. Every one of you is a priest before Me," saith the Lord.

This was the message, but instead of spreading it, we made a club, and we closed it all up, and we said nobody could enter in. But God had other plans. He spoke through the prophet Jeremiah, saying, "It has now reached the point where I'm granting Israel a bill of divorcement. She is no longer My wife; I am no longer her husband. I am no longer her father. I have broken My covenant with Israel. That which was bound together, I have now broken. I'm calling unto Myself a new people, in whom I will write My laws, My Scriptures, My commandments upon their hearts of flesh, not upon hearts of stone."

But the message given to Isaiah fell on ears that did not hear, eyes that did not see, and hearts that could not understand.

Woes were pronounced upon Ephraim and Jerusalem, especially for trusting in foreign nations and foreign alliances. The Lord said, "The only alliance you are to have is with Me. You are not to ally yourself with anybody else. I have led you; I have delivered you. I have been your God, your King, your Father. I have gone before you in all things. You're not to ally yourself with Egypt, with Assyria, with Babylon, with any other nation. If you put your trust in any other nation, you have pulled your trust away from Me. And if you pull your trust away from Me, I will not go before you."

The Lord spoke to Isaiah, saying, "I want you to give this message to My people and to the world. I am giving them My promise that I am bringing forth a righteous king, one in whom they can trust. And I promised I would also give them an outpouring of My Holy Spirit." This righteous King who was coming upon the face of the earth would be lifted up, He would be exalted, and the wilderness would be turned into a garden of the Lord.

Isaiah was sent by the Lord to go to speak to King Hezekiah, saying, "Thus saith the Lord, 'You'd better set your house in order, for you're about to die.'" And Hezekiah, being an old prayer warrior who knew how to pray to the Lord, turned into the corner, where his mind was focused upon the Lord and nobody else. He was not going to be distracted. He went into his prayer closet, and he said, "Lord, what good is it going to do You if You put me six feet under? I'm the only guy left in all of Israel that knows how to praise You, that knows how to glorify You, that knows how to lift up Your holy name. Nobody else is praising You or thanking You. They're all tied up with idolatry, with sorcery, with witchcraft. I'm the only one left. What good is it going to do You if I'm six feet under?"

Isaiah was on his way out, still in the courtyard of King Hezekiah, when the Lord spoke to him and told him, "Hey, Isaiah! Go back and tell good old King Hezekiah I've just heard his prayer, and I've already answered it. Tell him I've decided that he's got another fifteen years to live."

After Isaiah had told him the good news, Hezekiah, being a good Jew, said to Isaiah, "Give me a sign. How do I know the Lord spoke to you?"

Isaiah said to Hezekiah, "Well, you see that sundial in the courtyard of Ahaz? Would you like the Lord to move the time ahead ten degrees—forty minutes?"

Hezekiah replied, "Anybody can do that. I can move time ahead forty minutes. Time moves ahead all along. But if the Lord truly spoke to you, have Him move time backward ten degrees—forty minutes."

Isaiah prayed to the Lord, the Lord stopped the entire universe, and the sundial in the courtyard of Ahaz moved back ten degrees, forty minutes. He had received his sign.

Hezekiah lived exactly fifteen years to the day from the time when the Lord gave him the message. During the fifteen-year period, Hezekiah fathered Manasseh. At Hezekiah's death, his son Manasseh ascended the throne and became the longest reigning monarch of the throne of Judah or Israel. He ruled for fifty-seven years—and he was about the worst ruler the kingdom ever had.

It was through that line that God kept the promise

that He gave to David. He had said that through David would come an everlasting kingdom, and a king who would personally live forever. Manasseh was the one to whom the Lord kept constantly sending Isaiah, bringing the same message over and over again, "Repent, for the kingdom of God is at hand."

Manasseh did not like the message that Isaiah brought to him, so he had him sawn in half. Isaiah died a martyr's death to the Lord.

Zachariah too, died a martyr, because the Israelites didn't like his message. He was brought into the house of the Lord and killed, right before the ark of the covenant.

This is why the Lord holds Jerusalem and the people of Israel guilty for shedding the blood of His prophets.

In the second part of the life of obedience of Isaiah, there are predictions, warnings, and promises which refer to events beyond the captivity. Since Isaiah appeared on the scene some eight hundred years before Christ, and the kingdom of Israel was destroyed in 721 B.C., the people of Israel in the northern kingdom still had almost eighty years in which to repent. The kingdom of Judah wasn't destroyed until 586 B.C., so they had a little longer time. The same message was given to them.

The second portion of the prophecy of Isaiah is especially rich in messianic references. The key word in the entire book of Isaiah is salvation—Jesus. (Anytime you see the word "salvation" or "saved" in English, in Hebrew it is the name of Jesus, Yeshua.)

In Isaiah 12:3 we read, "Therefore with joy shall you draw water out of the wells of salvation—therefore with joy shall you draw water out of the wells of Jesus." He said, "I'm going to give you springs of living water." Here then, is a promise to you and me that with joy we will draw wells of water out of Him, a spring of living water.

In Isaiah 25:9 we see, "And it shall be said in that

day, 'Lo, this is our God; we have waited for Him, and He will save us: this is the Lord; we will be glad and we will rejoice in His salvation." We will rejoice in His salvation that He gives us, because He is the only way that we can receive eternal life.

In Isaiah 26:1 we find, "In that day shall this song be sung in the land of Judah; We have a strong city; salvation will God appoint for walls and bulwarks." Who will be the walls and bulwarks? Who will be the defense? Who will be the surrounding flame and fire? Who will be the one who will give us His divine protection? Jesus! Salvation will be appointed for us as our wall and our bulwark. Jesus Christ Himself.

In 45:17 is another great gift that God has given to you and me: "But Israel shall be saved in the Lord with an everlasting salvation—Israel shall be Jesus in the Lord with an everlasting salvation—and if you put your trust in Him, you shall not be ashamed nor confounded world without end."

In 49:8 is still another great promise that God gives to us. All these promises the Lord spoke through the prophet Isaiah: "Thus saith the Lord, 'In an acceptable time have I heard you, and in a day of salvation have I helped you: and I will preserve you, and I will give you for a covenant of the people, to establish the earth, to cause to inherit the desolate heritages.'"

The Lord says you will be a witness for Him. In all the ends of the earth, He will use you as a means and as a living witness for Him to cause other people to receive salvation.

In 52:7 is the promise, "How beautiful upon the mountains are the feet of Him that brings good tidings, that publishes peace; that brings good tidings, that publishes salvation; that saith unto Zion, 'Your God reigneth!'"

Jesus is upon the throne; He's still the same yesterday, today, and forever. He has not changed, He will not change, and He says, "I the Lord thy God, I do not change. I am still the same." So He's still sitting upon the throne. Praise God.

In 59:16 is another promise that God gave us through Isaiah as He spoke to him: "And He saw that there was no man, and (the Lord) wondered that there was no intercessor. Therefore His arm brought salvation unto Him, and His righteousness, it sustained him." By the righteousness of Jesus Christ, we were sustained. By the righteousness of Jesus Christ, salvation was brought unto us. We did not deserve it, but He looked beyond our fault. He saw our need. We did not merit it. We did not earn it. There was no way we could receive it. It was a gift from God. ("Charismatic" means gift of God.) He gives us a gift beyond our understanding.

Isaiah 59:17 sounds like the New Testament: "For He put on righteousness as a breastplate, and an helmet of salvation upon His head; He put on the garments of vengeance for clothing, and was clad with zeal as a cloke." This is our promise that this is what Jesus would be, this is what He would do.

Looking further, at 61:10: "I will greatly rejoice in the Lord, my soul shall be joyful in my God; for He has clothed me with the garments of salvation; He has covered me with the robe of righteousness, as a bridegroom decks himself with ornaments, and as a bride adorns herself with her jewels." He has done it to us. We can't do it, but He does it all.

In 62:1: "For Zion's sake will I not hold My peace, and for Jerusalem's sake I will not rest, until the righteousness thereof go forth as brightness. He will come into the world and say, 'I am the light of the world. Before Abraham was, I am.' And the salvation thereof, He will be as a lamp that burns." What happens when a lamp burns? He's going to take a little bit of garbage out of our life, isn't He? He's going to take some chaff, some dross—He's going to take it right out of our life.

In the third part of Isaiah, seven everlastings are revealed to us.

In 26:4: "Trust you in the Lord forever, for in the

Lord Jehovah is everlasting strength." If you're ever going to receive everlasting strength, you're going to receive it from the Lord. The joy of the Lord is the strength of our life.

The next everlasting is in 33:14: "The sinners in Zion are afraid; fearfulness hath surprised the hypocrites. Who among us shall dwell with the devouring fire? Who among us shall dwell with everlasting burnings?"

There's the promise of judgment at the same time as the promise of salvation. The Lord says you can choose whom you will serve. Joshua, in his phenomenon of obedience, stood up and said, "As for me and my house, this day will we choose the Lord." The Lord says we're going to have to make a choice. In these end times, we're going to have to stand up and be counted.

The third everlasting is in Isaiah 35:10: "And the ransomed of the Lord shall return, and come to Zion with songs and everlasting joy upon their heads: they shall obtain joy and gladness, and sorrow and sighing shall flee away from them because they will be in Christ Jesus." This is our promise: the everlasting joy of the Lord.

In Isaiah 45:17 God promises that Israel shall be saved in the Lord with an everlasting salvation, that you shall not be afraid nor confounded world without end.

In 54:8 the Lord says, "In a little wrath I hid My face from you for a moment; but with everlasting kindness will I have mercy on you, saith the Lord your Redeemer." Who is your redeemer? Jesus Christ. He said, "My wrath was just a little bit, and I hid My face from you for just a moment, but," He says, "now take a look." See the difference between the mercy, the kindness, the longsuffering, the graciousness of the Lord, as compared with the judgment of the Lord. He says, "Yes, I have put you into judgment. I have found you guilty, and yes, My wrath was upon you— but for just a moment. But with everlasting kindness will I have mercy on you," saith the Lord your Redeemer. Not kindness just for a short while. Everlasting kindness.

In 55:3 the Lord makes a covenant: "Come, incline your ear, and come unto me." In the Hebrew, when He says, "Incline your ear," He means that you are to take that stiffnecked arrogance that you have and bend it so you can hear what He's talking to you about. "Come unto me; hear and your soul shall live. And I will make an everlasting covenant with you, even the sure mercies of David. Even the mercies and the promises that I gave to David are yours."

What made David great was that the Lion of Judah would come from David. Jesus would be called the son of David.

In Isaiah 60:16, the Lord gives us another everlasting promise, an end-time prophecy: "The sun shall no more be your light by day; neither for brightness shall the moon give light unto you: but the Lord, the Lord Jesus Christ, shall be unto you an everlasting light and your God your glory."

In the Second Coming of Jesus, He will be our everlasting light. We will have no further need of the sun and the moon, because we will be in the radiance of Jesus Himself. We will be there worshiping and praising the Lord for a thousand years together in a song of praise and thanksgiving. We will say, "Glory to the lamb of God who sacrificed Himself to take away our sin."

The greatest promise given to us in Isaiah is in chapter 53, that Jesus did bear our sins and transgressions and our iniquities, and the chastisement necessary for us to obtain our peace was upon Him, and by His stripes we have already been healed in every area of our life, spiritually, mentally, emotionally, and physically. The Lord says He has already done it on the cross of Calvary. When He was upon the things for all mankind. Salvation is of the Lord. It is finished."

We don't have to stay in the wilderness that some of

us find ourselves in. *All we have to do is start praising and thanking Jesus for what He did for us, and if we stand and see the salvation of the Lord, if we will be still and know that He is God, we will find ourselves out of that circumstance, out of that trial, out of that tribulation, because the Lord says, "I do inhabit the praises of My people."*

So I say, *Praise God that He has given us all of these promises, that we have seventy-seven hundred promises in the Bible, and I claim every one of them. And the Lord says, "I have also given you fifteen hundred promises in the Bible in regard to healing. They're all yours. Take them. They're a gift. Just appropriate them, receive them. They're yours, but you have to stand by faith. And by faith you stand and see the salvation of the Lord. By your obedience unto Me," saith the Lord, "I will show you the salvation of the Lord. I will go before you. I will prepare the way. That crooked road that you happen to be on right now, I will straighten out for you, for it is I, Jesus, Who goes before you."*

Isaiah gives us a very beautiful portrait of Christ, throughout the book. In Isaiah 7:14, the Lord gives a promise: "Therefore the Lord Himself shall give you a sign; Behold, a virgin shall conceive, and bear a son, and shall call his name Immanuel." Immanuel, in the Hebrew, means "God with us in the flesh."

Rabbis have disputed for years that the word "virgin" was put in there by Christians and not by Jews, that the Christian people corrupted the Hebrew. Now the Hebrew word in Isaiah 7:14 is *almah,* "that an *almah* shall conceive." An *almah* is a woman. The word for "virgin" in Hebrew is *bethula.*

Let us look at an episode in the Old Testament that makes the distinction clear:

Abraham sent his trusted servant, Eliezer, to go back to the land of his kindred to bring back a bride for Isaac. Eliezer set a fleece before the Lord. He said, "Lord God of Abraham, if You have shown me mercy and mercy toward my master, how am I going to know what woman to pick out for my master's son?" He said, "I'm asking You for a sign. The sign I'm asking for is that the first person, the first woman, the first girl, the first virgin that comes along, and I ask her for a drink of water, she will say, 'I will give you a drink of water, and I will also draw a drink for your camels, too."

He had ten camels with him, and each camel would drink thirty gallons of water. The woman was going to have to draw three hundred gallons of water. That's a pretty good fleece, isn't it?

Rebecca came along, and Eliezer asked her for a drink. She said, "Okay, I'll give you a drink, and I'll also draw water for your camels."

And Eliezer prostrated himself before the Lord, and he started worshiping the Lord, and he said, "Thank You, Lord. You have been faithful to my master, Abraham. You have prepared the way for me, and I know now she is the right person."

The word used for Rebecca in the Hebrew at this point is *bethula*. She was a virgin. When Eliezer told her about Isaac, she gave her consent. She would become espoused, engaged, to Isaac. Eliezer took a ring and put it in her nose to designate she was now espoused. He went home with her in the afternoon; he spoke to Laban, her brother. He spoke to her father. They gave their consent; she was a virgin of consentable age, and the word in the Hebrew changed from *bethula* to *almah*. She was still a virgin, but the word designated that she had become engaged to a man.

The Lord specified, "Therefore, the Lord Himself will give you a sign that this virgin who will conceive will be a virgin who will be espoused to a man called Joseph."

The great ceremony in the Hebrew till today with Orthodox Jews is the engagement, not the marriage ceremony. The marriage ceremony just consummates the marriage. Once an Orthodox Jew signs the marriage contract, and the espousal and the engagement takes place, from that point on, they cannot simply call off the engagement. It takes a regular divorce proceeding.

Did you ever stop to wonder why Joseph, in the New Testament, when he found out that Mary was with child, had sought to put her away privately, since she was only engaged to him? He could have had her stoned to death. Being espoused to him, she was married to him, but the marriage was not consummated. And the Lord specified exactly that she would be a virgin who would be engaged. The Lord Himself gave that sign.

In Isaiah 11:1, we see of what family He would come: "There shall come forth a rod out of the stem of Jesse, and a Branch shall grow out of his roots." Jesus would be from the house and branch of Jesse.

And the Lord promised that the seven manifold spirit would rest upon this Branch from the root of Jesse. In Isaiah 11:2, we read: "And the spirit of the Lord shall rest upon Him, the spirit of wisdom and understanding, the spirit of counsel and might, the spirit of knowledge and of the fear—the reverence—of the Lord." The seven manifold spirit of the Holy Spirit would rest upon Christ Jesus. This was His anointing.

Jesus' mission was described in Isaiah 9:2: "The people that walked in darkness have seen a great light: they that dwell in the land of the shadow of death, upon them has the light shined." That would be His mission, that people who had walked in darkness would see a great light, Jesus Christ. That they who dwelt in the land of the shadow of death would have the light of Christ shine upon them. That would be His mission.

Another part of His mission was described in 11:3: "And the Lord shall make Him of quick understanding in the fear of the Lord." In Hebrew, the word "fear" really means, "the fear of the Lord is to see the Lord." If you see the Lord, you revere Him, you respect Him, you stand in awe of Him. The book of Proverbs tells us that the fear of the Lord is the beginning of wisdom. The seeing of the Lord, the reverence of the Lord, the standing in awe of the Lord, is the beginning of wisdom and the beginning of knowledge. To see Him is to know Him, and to see Him, to know Him, is to love Him.

The Lord shall make Him of quick understanding in the fear of the Lord, and He shall not judge after the sight of His eyes, neither reprove after the hearing of His ears. He will never return evil for evil, and He will teach us to do the very same thing. He will constantly say, "Father, forgive them, for they know not what they do." And we are to do the very same thing.

"Father, forgive that person who has just now put a knife in my back and just torn me to shreds. He doesn't know what he's doing. Now I'm going to pray for him."

Jesus said, "I gave you ten living words on Mount Sinai." In the Hebrew, they're not called commandments, they're called the ten living words. And Jesus said, "I did not come into the world to break a commandment, but to fulfill them. And to make it a little easier for you, I'll reduce the number of commandments to two. The first one is to love your God with all your heart, your soul, and your mind." (Deut. 6:5; cf. Mark 12:29-30)

The soul is the will, the intellect, and the emotion. Jesus told us to love God with all our will. Can you love the Lord your God with all your intellect? Can you bypass your intellect and love Him in spite of your intellect? Can you get emotional about God, and stand and lift your hands in song, or praise, or thanksgiving? Can you get emotional about God? Love the Lord your God with all your heart and soul and mind?

Jesus said, "The second commandment, which is like unto the first is that you shall not bear a grudge or a resentment against your neighbor, but you shall love your neighbor as yourself" (Lev. 19:18).

When I used to get up in the mornings to shave, I used to look in the mirror and see absolute perfection. I saw the most perfect person alive, and I rationalized and I forgave myself for everything. Then one day the Lord spoke to me. He said, "Michael, you see the way you excuse yourself, and you rationalize for yourself, and you see the perfection in yourself? That's the way I want you to love your neighbor. Now you can do the same for him. This is what I mean by loving your neighbor as you love yourself. The way you forgive and excuse yourself, forgive him the very same way."

And then the Lord said, "A new commandment I give you, that you love one another the way I have loved you." (John 13:34)

And then He spoke to Peter about obedience: "Pete, do you love Me?" Peter said, "Sure, Lord, I love You." He said, "Feed My lambs." And then He said, "Simon, do you really love Me?" He said, "Yeah, Lord, I love You." He said, "Feed My sheep." Then, Peter's name being Jacob in Hebrew, Jesus said, "Jacob, do you really love Me?" He said, "Lord, for crying out loud, I do love You. What do You keep on asking me for?" He said, "Feed My sheep."

Then He asked, "Can you be obedient unto Me even if it means your death?"

And Peter told Him, "I will go wherever You go. I'll drink of the same cup. I'll even die for You."

It was the eve of the Passover, and they had just had the last supper together. Jesus said to Peter, "Before this night is over, you're going to deny Me three times."

And Peter said, "Me? I'll never deny You, never. It'll never happen." I will not deny you in any wise. (Mark 14:31)

After Jesus was taken prisoner, they came to Peter and said, "Didn't we see you with that man Jesus?"

He said, "Me? I never heard of Him."

And they said, "But you speak with a Galilean accent."

"Oh," he said, "that's something I picked up on my travels to Israel." And then again he was confronted, and the third time he denied the Lord. This was Peter the chicken-hearted.

Later, the Lord told him, "I want you to wait in Jerusalem until I ascend, and I will send you back another One who will give you power from on high. He will give you the dynamite. (The word in Greek is *dunamis*.) He will plug you in, because it will be Me in My Holy Spirit. When you receive this power from on high, you will know, understand, and perceive everything that I have told you. It will all be brought to life."

Peter, now the lion, stood up before thousands of Jews who were in Jerusalem worshiping the Lord on the Day of Pentecost, fifty days after Passover.

Fifty days after the exodus from Egypt, God, on Mount Sinai, had spoken to the Jews and given them the ten living words, the Ten Commandments. And the blood was sprinkled upon us in an everlasting covenant relationship with Him, and He had promised, "If you will be obedient unto Me, I will never leave you, I will never forsake you, and I will never fail you." The Jews still observe the festival of Pentecost, when God gave them the commandments.

So Jews from all over the world were in Jerusalem worshiping at the festival of Pentecost when Peter the lionhearted, baptized in the Holy Spirit, full of the Holy Spirit, stood up and started preaching the message from Abraham clear on to Jesus Christ. Three thousand of his hearers received Christ that very same day, and the Holy Spirit fell upon them. We praise God for this miracle.

In Isaiah 11:4 we see that Christ's mission would include His being a judge and a reprover: "With righteousness shall He judge the poor, and He will reprove with equity for the meek of the earth. He shall smite the earth with the rod of His mouth, and with the breath of His lips shall He slay the wicked." Those who would not repent would die in their impenitence. He still gives the very same message that He spoke to Moses in Exodus 34. He says, "I will never forgive the guilty." How do you remain guilty? By not accepting the sacrifice of Jesus Christ, by not repenting before the Lord.

Jesus would also be a lawgiver: "He shall not fail

nor be discouraged, till He have set judgment in the earth: and the isles of the sea shall wait for His law." (Isa 42:4) The isles of the sea are all the western nations, including the United States. They shall wait for the law of Jesus Christ, as He fulfills the law for each and every one of us.

Again, He would be a liberator: "He will come willingly to open the blind eyes, to bring out the prisoners from the prison, and those that sit in darkness out of the prison house." He would set them free as He sets us free.

Another part of Jesus' mission was that He would be the burden-bearer (53:4). Many of us like to play the part of Jesus Christ. We all like to carry our own burdens. Why do you do it when the Lord says He will do it for you?

Surely He has borne our griefs. Why should we grieve if He will carry that burden for us? He has already carried our sorrows, yet we did esteem Him stricken, smitten of God, and afflicted.

Another part of Jesus' mission was to bear our sins (Isa. 53:6): "All we like sheep have gone astray; we have turned every one to his own way; and the Lord has laid on Him the iniquity of us all." He took our sins, our transgressions, and our iniquities.

In Isaiah 53:12 we see that He will be our intercessor, that He will intercede for us. God said, "He was numbered with the transgressors; and He bore the sin of many, and made intercession for the transgressors." The word "transgressors" refers to those who have willfully and deliberately sinned against us. Jesus makes intercession for them, because the Scripture tells us He came into the world, tempted on all points like we are.

And He says, "Yes, Michael, I know where you were tempted, and I went through it Myself, and now I'm interceding for you. Come to Me and ask for forgiveness, and I will forgive you."

We see also in Isaiah 53:5 that Jesus is the only Savior. "He was wounded for our transgressions; He was bruised for our iniquities: the chastisement of our peace was upon Him; and with His stripes we were and are healed."

In the Book of Isaiah, several titles are given to Jesus by the Word of the Lord and by the Holy Spirit. In 7:14, He's called Immanuel, God with us. And in Isaiah 9:6, He is called the mighty God, the everlasting Father, the Prince of Peace: "For unto us a child is born, unto us a son is given: and the government shall be upon His shoulder, and His name shall be called Wonderful, Counsellor, The Mighty God, The Everlasting Father, The Prince of Peace. Of the increase of His government and peace there shall be no end, upon the throne of David, and upon His kingdom, to order it, and to establish it with judgment and with justice from henceforth even forevermore." These are His titles.

In 32:1, we see that He is the righteous king: "Behold, a king shall reign in righteousness, and princes shall rule in judgment."

In 42:1, we see that He is the divine servant. The Hebrew people missed the fact that Christ would come as a suffering servant. They expected Him to appear in glory and deliver Israel out of the hands of the Romans. But listen to what the Word of the Lord says:

"Behold My servant, whom I uphold; My elect, in whom My soul delights; I have put My Holy Spirit upon Him. He shall bring forth judgment to the Gentiles, to the heathen." He would come as a suffering servant, but He would be a divine servant.

In 53:1, we see that He is the arm of the Lord: "Who has believed our report? And to whom is the arm of the Lord revealed?"

The Messiah would also be an anointed preacher. Isaiah 61:1-2 was quoted by Jesus in Luke 4:18-19: "The Spirit of the Lord God is upon Me; because the Lord has anointed Me to preach good tidings unto the meek; He has sent Me to bind up the brokenhearted, to proclaim liberty to the captives, and the opening of the prison to them that are bound; to proclaim the acceptable year of the Lord."

When Jesus was baptized in the river Jordan by John the Baptist, the heavens opened and the dove of the Holy Spirit descended upon Him, and a voice came from heaven saying, "This is My beloved son in whom I am well pleased."

Then Jesus was led, full of the Holy Spirit, into the wilderness of Judaea to be tempted of the devil. He defeated the devil, and He was still full of and controlled by the Holy Spirit. He went back to Nazareth as was His custom on the sabbath day. He walked in; He was a respected rabbi. They asked Him to come up and read the Scripture. He was handed the scroll of Isaiah, and by divine appointment, it was opened to the sixty-first chapter of Isaiah. Jesus stopped reading when He came to, "the day of vengeance of our God," because that referred to His Second Coming.

After reading, He sat down, and the eyes of all those in the synagogue of Nazareth were upon Him. "Today," He said, "you have seen this prophecy fulfilled before your very eyes."

In 63:1 we see that He is a mighty traveler: "Who is this that cometh from Edom, with dyed garments from Bozrah? This that is glorious in His apparel, traveling in the greatness of His strength? I that speak in righteousness, mighty to save." He had come to save the entire world.

All of these are portraits of Christ.

Now the characteristics and the gifts that He has operating within Him we see also in Isaiah. He has the spirit of wisdom (11:2). He has spiritual discernment (11:3). He has justice (11:4). He has the righteousness of the Lord (11:5).

In Isaiah 42:2, the Lord told what would happen to Him when He was taken captive and brought in before the high priest: "He shall not cry nor lift up nor cause His voice to be heard in the street." He would go willingly to the cross.

The same thought appears also in Isaiah 53:7: "He was oppressed, He was afflicted, yet He opened not His mouth. He is brought as a lamb to the slaughter, and as a sheep before his shearers is dumb, so He opened not His mouth." He was obedient unto His death that He might save us.

We see in 53:10 His vicarious atonement: "Yet it pleased the Lord to bruise Him; for He has put Him to grief: when thou shalt make His soul an offering for sin, He shall see His seed, He shall prolong His days, and the pleasure of the Lord shall prosper in His hand."

We see his suffering in 52:14: "As many were astonied at thee; His visage was so marred more than any man, and His form more than the sons of men." And in 53:9, we see that He made His grave with the wicked and with the rich in His death although He had done no violence, neither was there any deceit in His mouth.

In 53:12, we see His greatness, that the Lord would divide Him a portion with the great.

In 53:11: "He shall see the travail of His soul, and He shall be satisfied; by His knowledge shall my righteous servant justify many, for He shall bear their iniquities."

There is a saving power. He will justify you and me. "Justify" means that it will be just-as-if-I'd never sinned, just as if you'd never sinned, because He would bear our sins, our transgressions, and our iniquity.

Praise the Lord that God gave us this great message through the obedience of the great prophet Isaiah, and that even the message about His Second Coming is in the Book of Isaiah. The Lord has already revealed to us what is going to take place.

What about our obedience? How do we stand with the Lord? Are there any of us holding a grudge, a resentment against anybody right now? Is that obedience unto the Lord?

The Lord says, "Can you come into My house and pray a prayer that I taught you to pray, saying, 'Our Father, who art in heaven, hallowed be Thy name, Thy kingdom come, Thy will be done in earth as it is in heaven. Give me this day my daily bread, and now I want You to hold a grudge against me, as I'm holding a grudge against my fellowman'?" Is that the way He taught us to pray? Or, "Lord, forgive me of my debts as I forgive my debtors. Forgive me of my trespasses as I forgive those who trespass against me."

If you are holding a grudge, a resentment, against anybody, you cannot possibly come into the house of the Lord and pray the Lord's prayer and mean it.

He says, "Take that log out of your eye. Will you look at that little speck on that eyelash in your neighbor's eye? You've got a big log in your own eye."

Any time you judge or criticize, whom are you really judging and criticizing? Yourself. Usually, the thing that we judge and criticize in other people is something we are hung up on ourselves. The Scripture tells us that our judgment will come as an arrow right back to us and judge us. The way we have judged others is the way we will be judged.

The Lord has shown each and every one of us His love, His grace, and His mercy. And He says, "If you'll permit this love and this grace and this mercy that I have shown to you to flow from your life to somebody else's life, it will touch them, and by your love they will come to know My love and believe that I live, that I'm still alive, that I'm still in the business of transforming people. That I still save, that I still deliver and I still heal."

Praise the Lord that Christ was obedient unto death, that we who believe in Him will never perish but have everlasting life.

Praise God!

12

Daniel

(Daniel 1-12)

Every chapter of the Bible will speak to you about obedience. In these end times, the Lord is preparing His bride, as the Bridegroom is coming back for His Body of believers. And it is by our obedience that we are going to be prepared.

The phenomenon of obedience was at work in the life of Daniel, the statesman and prophet. The name Daniel in Hebrew, means "God is my judge, God is the defender of my right."

We know nothing of Daniel's family, except that he was a descendant of the royal house of David. He was carried away captive to Babylon during the reign of Jehoiakim.

There is a very marked resemblance between Daniel's life and that of Joseph. Both were carried away captive in their youth. Both were model young men. Joseph was seventeen; Daniel was seventeen. Both found employment in a king's court, by divine appointment. Both became interpreters of dreams. The interpretations were given to them by the Lord. Through this gift from God, both were exalted to rulership—Daniel in Babylon, Joseph in Egypt. Both lived pure lives in the midst of corrupt courts, and both died in foreign lands. Both were very unjustly persecuted, their hardships becoming stepping stones to honor. God used both of them for a witness and a testimony, to teach obedience to His people.

If you and I have a hardship in our life, a test, a trial, a tribulation, the Lord is using it to clean out some garbage. He's cleaning out some dross, some chaff. He's teaching us to stand, to praise Him in all circumstances, and to say, "Yes, Lord. I don't like the circumstance that I'm in, but I'm going to thank You for it anyway. Because You told me in Your Word that all things will work together for my good, if only I will let You do it. That's the key. I have to be obedient unto You, Lord. I have to let You do it. I'll let You be Jesus. I'm not going to play Your part."

Jesus is the greatest garbage collector in the world. All we have to do is release our garbage to Him, our grudges, our resentments, our hatreds, our needs, our burdens. He says, "Bring them to Me. Let Me take them from you. Why should you carry them? I have already healed you. I have already delivered you. I have already saved you. By My stripes on My back, you have been healed in every area of your life."

The main theme in the Book of Daniel is the sovereignty of God over the affairs of men in all ages. The pagan king's confession of this fact constitutes a key verse in the Book of Daniel:

The king answered unto Daniel, and said, "Of a truth, your God is a God of gods and a Lord of kings, and a revealer of secrets, seeing you have been able to reveal this secret unto me." He had received the interpretation of a dream through Daniel, and the king acknowledged that God is the living God. His heathen idol, made with his own hands, couldn't give him an answer.

The Book of Daniel contains an account of thrilling events and divine intervention unsurpassed anywhere in the Old Testament, as God revealed His purpose and His plan to Daniel.

Daniel, like Moses, was both a statesman and a prophet. As a seer—another word in the Hebrew for prophet—through the power of the Holy Spirit, he was given a telescopic vision which had a longer range than most of the other prophets put together. The Lord gave him a vision of the end times. Jesus gave a vision of the Book of Revelation to John, and Daniel was given almost the very same vision. Daniel and Revelation go together. You really cannot separate the two books. They bear witness one to another.

Daniel saw beyond the coming of Christ, and beheld Him in His enthronement as King of kings. He saw His Second Coming, when He would be King of kings and Lord of lords, when every knee should bow and every tongue confess that Jesus Christ is Lord. Daniel was particularly the prophet of the last days.

Jeremiah had told the people of Judah that they had sinned, that they had rejected the living God by their disobedience. Over six hundred two thousand of them had to die in the wilderness because they had failed to give the honor and the praise and the glory to the Lord. They constantly murmured and griped. The Lord had put them into one captivity after another, but still they refused to listen to Him. And then the Lord promised that if they would voluntarily go into captivity and exile, after seventy years they could rebuild the temple that Nebuchadnezzar had destroyed.

The king of Babylon, knowing through sorcery and witchcraft that the Lord had given a promise to King David that from him would be coming a king who would personally live forever and a kingdom which would last forever, sought to destroy the coming Messiah by castrating Daniel, Shadrach, Meschach, and Abednego, all four princes of the house of David. But he overlooked one, Zerubbabel. When the exile was over, Zerubbabel would be the first one to lead back the group of captives who, the Lord promised, would be released by a man who had not even been born yet—Cyrus. The Lord named him by name: "In the future is coming a man whom I will use as My servant, and his name is Cyrus." God, knowing the beginning, the middle, and the ending, can call a man's name way in the future. Cyrus would conquer Babylon; he would set the captives free and send them back home.

The enemy always knows when there is a deliverer, a prophet, a Savior, coming. They knew through the power of the enemy that Christ would be coming from the line of Judah, King David's line, but they overlooked Zerubbabel.

So Daniel went back to his house and made the thing known to Meshach, Shadrach, and Abednego that they might intercede in prayer, that they might ask mercy of the God of heaven concerning the secret, that Daniel and his companions should not perish with the rest of the wise men, the magicians of Nebuchadnezzar. The four of them prayed all night long, that the secret might be revealed to Daniel. It came in a vision in the night, just before the dawn.

Then Daniel blessed the God of heaven in one of the most beautiful songs of praise found in the Bible. Daniel said, "Blessed be the name of God from everlasting unto everlasting, for wisdom and might are His." Daniel did not take the praise, and the honor, and the glory from God, or from Jesus Christ to himself. He praised God, because he knew that He alone is Lord of lords and King of kings.

And Daniel continued, saying, "He changes the times and the seasons. He removeth kings and setteth up kings. He giveth wisdom unto the wise and knowledge to them that know understanding. He revealeth the deep and secret things. He knoweth what is in the darkness, and the light, who is Jesus Christ, was in the very beginning, and He dwells with Him. In the beginning was God, and the Word was God, and the Word still remains God.

"I thank Thee, and I praise Thee, O Thou God of my fathers, who hast given me wisdom and might and hast now made known unto me what we desired of Thee, for Thou hast now made known unto us the king's matter."

Then Daniel went to Arioch whom the king had appointed to destroy all the wise men of Babylon. He said unto him, "Destroy not the wise men of Babylon. Bring me in before the king, and I will declare unto the king the interpretation."

Arioch brought Daniel before the king in haste, and the king asked, "Are you able to make known unto me the dream which I have seen and the interpretation thereof?"

And Daniel answered the king and said, "The secret which the king has asked can neither wise men, magicians, enchanters, or astrologers declare unto the king. But there is a God in heaven that reveals secrets, and He has made known to King Nebuchadnezzar what shall be in the end of days." As Daniel continued speaking, he said, "As for you, O King, as you lay upon your bed, thoughts came into your mind about what should come to pass hereafter; and He who reveals secrets was making known to you what will come to pass. But as for me, this secret is not revealed to me for any wisdom that I have more than anyone living, but in order that the interpretation may be made known to the king, that you may know the thoughts of your heart and of your mind.

"You, O King, you saw and you beheld a great image. This image which was mighty and of exceedingly great brightness stood before you, and the appearance of it was frightening and terrible. Its head was of fine gold, its breast and its arms of silver, its belly and its thighs of bronze, its legs of iron, its feet part of iron and part of burned potter's clay. And as you looked, a stone was cut out without human hand which smote the image on its feet, which were of iron and clay, and the burnt clay of the potter, and broke them to pieces. Then was the iron, the burnt potter's clay, the bronze, the silver, the gold, broken and crushed together and became like the chaff of the summer threshingfloors, and the wind carried them away, so that not a trace of them could be found. And the stone, the rock that smote the image, became a great mountain and filled the whole earth."

This Rock was the Rock of Ages, Jesus Christ Himself. It was the very same Rock that followed the people of Israel in the wilderness for forty years and supplied them with living water that they would not perish, but that they would constantly drink of that living water, as God tried to bring them back to obedience and to salvation.

Daniel said to the king, "This was the dream, and we will now tell the interpretation of it to the king. You, O King, are the king of the earthly kings to whom the God of heaven has given the kingdom, the power, the might, and the glory. Wherever the children of men dwell, the beasts of the field, and the birds of the heavens, He has given unto your hands, and He has made you to rule over them all. You, King of Babylon are the head of gold. But after you shall rise another kingdom (the Medo-Persian), which will be inferior to and earthward from you; and still a third kingdom of bronze (Greece under Alexander the Great), which shall bear rule over the earth; and the fourth kingdom (which will be Rome) shall be as strong as iron. Just as iron breaks into pieces and subdues and crushes all things, this kingdom shall break and crush all of these. And as you saw in the feet and the toes, part of potter's burnt clay and part of iron, it shall be a divided kingdom."

And the Lord revealed through Daniel other things which would come to pass. "And in the end times, shall the God of heaven set up a kingdom which shall never be destroyed nor shall the sovereignty be left to another people, but it shall break and crush and consume all other kingdoms and it shall stand forever. But just as you saw that the stone was cut out of the mountain without hands and that it broke in pieces, the iron, the bronze, the clay, the silver, the gold, the great God has made known to the king that it shall come to pass in the end times. The dream is certain and the interpretation of it is sure."

After Daniel had told him his dream and the interpretation of it, Nebuchadnezzar fell upon his face and paid homage to Daniel as a great prophet of the highest God, and he ordered that an offering of incense should be offered up in honor of this God. And the king answered Daniel and said, "Of a truth, your God is a God of gods, and a Lord of kings, and a revealer of secrets, seeing that you could reveal this secret and mystery through this Jesus Christ of yours."

Then the king made Daniel great. He gave him many great gifts. He made him to rule over the whole province of Babylon, and to be chief governor over all the wise men in Babylon. And Daniel requested of the king that he appoint Shadrach, Meshach, and Abednego over the affairs of the province of Babylon, but Daniel remained in the gate of the king at the king's court. Again, God had rewarded him for his obedience.

There were six moral conflicts in which Daniel and his companions would have to participate.

Sometimes you and I are going to have to participate in conflict, and you'll ask me the question, "Why? Didn't Jesus say, 'I came into the world to give you life, and to give it to you more abundantly?' Why do we have to be in any sort of a conflict?" Jesus also told us we must always be on guard against the triune forces of evil—the world, the flesh, and the devil. And Jesus said, "You can be in the world, but you don't have to be a part of it. I have set you apart. I have divinely ordained every one of you. You are all ministers and priests unto me. You are all epistles unto me. I have given you the authority that I gave Peter, James, and John," and He said, "I give you greater authority to do greater things than I have done Myself—if only you believe it." There's the key. He said, "If you have the faith of a mustard seed, you can command that mountain to move and it will move."

So Jesus said, "Ask the Father in My name, presenting all that I am to you, and you shall receive. Seek, and you will find. Knock, and it will be opened unto you." Ask, seek, knock. Put their initial letters together, and you have "ask."

The Lord says, "Ask." You have to humble yourself to ask, and He says you will receive, but you have to ask first. You can't just sit down and say, "Well, Lord, I'm out of a job, and I'm going to sit here in my house, and praise You all day. If You decide to give me a job, somebody will call me on the phone and offer it to me." Well, I'm sorry to tell you, it's not going to work that way. Jesus said, "Occupy until I come." So you go out and look for a job, and pray that the Lord will guide you to the right place. If you're committed unto Him, He will go before you and prepare the way for you, but you must be obedient unto Him first.

The first conflict that Daniel encountered was between pagan self-indulgence and conscientious abstinence in promoting health. He could indulge himself in the food and wine of paganism and idolatry, and he would not have any persecution in the early part of his life. He would not have to stand and see the salvation of the Lord. Everything would come his way if he put his trust and his refuge in Nebuchadnezzar, king of Babylon, instead of keeping it in the Lord. But Daniel chose to abstain, and he stood with the Lord and said, "Yes, Lord, I will stand and see Your salvation, and if I must be persecuted for Your sake, I will. My will is Your will, and Your will is my will." Daniel purposed in his heart that he would not defile himself with the king's dainties, nor with the wine which he drank. He was going to remain true to what God gave him.

Therefore, Daniel requested of the prince of the eunuchs that he might not defile himself. Now God had made Daniel to find kindness and compassion in the sight of the prince of the eunuchs. As the prince of eunuchs looked upon him, he saw not Daniel, but the grace of the Lord upon him. And the prince of the eunuchs said unto Daniel, "I fear my Lord, the king, who has appointed your food and your drink, for why should he see your face worse looking than the other youth who are of your own age? Would you endanger my head with the king? You're going to put me in a dangerous situation if you don't eat of the food and of the wine that he has placed aside for you."

Then said Daniel to the steward whom the prince of the eunuchs had appointed over them, "Prove your servants, I beseech you, ten days. Let them give us pulse to eat, water to drink. Then let our countenances be looked upon before you and the countenances of the youth that eat of the king's dainties, and as you see, deal with your servants. We're willing to trust the Lord. Give us that which is not the fanciest of all foods —give us pulse to eat." Pulse is almost like a cereal. "We'll live on that, and you can keep your dainties and your wine, the food from the king's table. The Lord says He will supply all of our needs, and we're going to trust Him. And after ten days, look upon our faces, and look upon the faces of the other youth." And the steward consented.

After the ten-day period, the steward saw that Daniel and his companions looked better, their countenances were fairer, and they were fatter in flesh than all the youth that did eat of the king's food. So the steward kept on taking away their meat and wine that they should drink, and he kept giving them pulse and fruit and vegetables.

For their obedience, God gave them some of the gifts of the Holy Spirit. After three years, when they were brought before the king, he found that God had given them wisdom and understanding—ten times more than all the magicians and astrologers that were in his realm. And so they were chosen to be the personal attendants of King Nebuchadnezzar.

By abstaining, by being obedient to the Lord, Daniel won the first conflict because he was trusting God.

The second conflict was between pagan magic and heavenly wisdom. In the second year of his reign, King Nebuchadnezzar had a dream which troubled him.

When he called on his magicians and astrologers and sorcerers for the interpretation of his dream, they couldn't give it to him—because he had forgotten what the dream was. Nevertheless, he told them that if they did not tell him what his dream had been, and give him the interpretation of it, he would have them cut in pieces. Furthermore, the king was so angry that he commanded that all of the wise men of Babylon be destroyed. This, of course, included Daniel, Meschach, Shadrach, and Abednego.

When Arioch, the captain of the king's guard, came to arrest Daniel, Daniel went to the king and promised that if he would give him just a little time, he would tell the king his dream and the interpretation of it.

Daniel could interpret dreams by pagan magic or by the heavenly wisdom of the Lord. He could ask the Lord, "Lord, give me the interpretation of this dream," or he could interpret the dream through pagan magic. Which way would he take—the way of Satan, or the way of the Lord? If he was moving in the flesh, he would take the way of pagan magic, and he would turn out to be a big hero. But if he took the way of the Lord, he would turn away all the people in the king's court.

Daniel chose to stand and say, "I am serving a living God, and I'm obedient unto Him. I'll not get involved in sorcery, witchcraft, Taro cards, Ouija boards, astrology, the signs of the zodiac. I'll not get involved in any of those things. I'll remain loyal to the living God."

The third conflict that came into Daniel's life was between heathen idolatry and loyalty to God: Now Nebuchadnezzar the king made an image of gold, whose height was threescore cubits, and the breadth thereof six cubits, and he set it up in the plain of Dura in the province of Babylon.

Then Nebuchadnezzar the king sent to gather together the satraps, the deputies, the governors, the judges, the treasurers, the counselors, the sheriffs, and all the rulers of the provinces to come to the dedication of the image which Nebuchadnezzar the king had set up.

Now all these people came together for the dedication, and they stood before the image that Nebuchadnezzar had set up. Then an herald cried aloud, "To you it is commanded, O people, nations, and languages, at what time you hear the sound of the cornet, flute, the harp, the sackbut, the psaltery, the dulcimer, all kinds of music, you shall fall down and worship the golden image that Nebuchadnezzar the king has set up.

"And whosoever shall not fall down and worship shall the same hour be cast into the midst of a burning fiery furnace."

Which way would you take? Would you gamble on going into a fiery furnace? Would you say to the Lord, "Lord, You gave me Your promise. You said to me that You would never leave me, nor forsake me. You said to me You would never fail me in any way whatsoever. So I will not fall down and worship this heathen image. I'm going to stand and be obedient unto You. I will not display the phenomenon of disobedience, but obedience, and I will trust that You will be with me if I am cast into that fiery furnace."

Are we willing to go with Jesus Christ into a fiery furnace? Jesus told us that if we intend to follow Him, we're going to have to take up our cross every day and follow Him. And He says, "Your born-again experience is a day-by-day and a minute-by-minute experience, because I am constantly working in your life." He will bring us to that point of perfection in Him, as He is now preparing His Body of believers for the coming of the Bridegroom. He's on His way back soon. And it is by our obedience that we enter into that Body of believers, that we become the bride.

If we are disobedient at the last moment, we are not going to have our lamps completely full with oil, and some of us are going to run to the store to get some more oil, and by the time we get back, we'll have missed it. He's going to have already come, and the rest of the Body of believers will be gone. We had better be prepared.

At the time when some people were worshiping the golden image, certain Chaldeans came near and brought accusations against the Jews. They said to Nebuchadnezzar, "King, you who live forever and ever, you're the one who made a decree that when every man shall hear the sound of the horn, the pipe, the harp, the psaltery—all kinds of music—they shall fall down and worship the golden image. And whoso does not fall down and worship the image should be cast into the midst of a burning fiery furnace. Now there are certain Jews whom you, king, have appointed over the affairs of the province of Babylon—Shadrach, Meshach, and Abednego—and these men, O king, they have not regarded you. They serve not your god, nor worship the golden image which you have set up."

Daniel was not involved in this fiery furnace conflict, because Nebuchadnezzar had sent him to another province to get him out of the way. He did not want to lose Daniel.

Nebuchadnezzar was filled with rage and fury, and he commanded Shadrach, Meshach, and Abednego to be brought before him. Nebuchadnezzar spoke to them and gave them an out. He said, "Is it true? Is it true, O Shadrach, Meshach, and Abednego, that you do not serve my god or worship the golden image which I have set up?

"Now if you are ready at the time you hear the sound of the horn, the pipe, the psaltery, and you do fall down and worship the image I have made, well— But if you do not worship, you will be cast in the very same hour into the midst of a burning fiery furnace, and who is the God that shall deliver you out of my hands?"

Shadrach, Meshach, and Abednego answered him and said to the king, "Nebuchadnezzar, we don't even have to concern our minds to answer thee in this matter. If our God, whom we serve, is able to deliver us, He will deliver us from the burning fiery furnace and out of your hands. But if not, let it be known unto you, O King, that we will not serve your god, nor worship the golden image which you have set up."

Then Nebuchadnezzar was filled with fury, and the form of his countenance, his face, was changed against Shadrach, Meshach, and Abednego. Then he spoke and commanded that they should heat the furnace seven times hotter than it was ordinarily heated, and he commanded the most mighty men that were in his army to bind Shadrach, Meshach, and Abednego and to cast them into the burning fiery furnace. They were bound in their cloaks, their tunics, their robes, and their other clothes, and they were cast into the midst of the fiery furnace.

As they were being cast into the fire, the fire was so hot that the men who were casting them into the fire were consumed by the fire. And Shadrach, Meshach, and Abednego, fell down, bound, into the midst of the burning fiery furnace.

Suddenly Nebuchadnezzar jumped up, alarmed. And he said, "Did we not cast three men bound into the midst of the fire?"

The onlookers answered, "Yes, King, it's true."

And he said, "Take a look! Do you see what I see? I see four men loose there. They were in chains, they were bound, they were tied, they were gagged—but all these things have fallen off. The men are loose, and they are walking in the midst of the fire! They have no hurt, and the appearance of the fourth is like the Son of God."

Jesus Christ Himself was walking with them in that fiery furnace. *"I will never leave you or forsake you."*

Then Nebuchadnezzar came near to the mouth of the burning fiery furnace, and he spoke and said, "Shadrach, Meshach, and Abednego, you servants of God most high, come forth and come here." Then Shadrach, Meshach, and Abednego came forth out of the midst of the fire. And everybody saw that the fire had no power over their bodies, nor was a hair of their heads singed, neither were their coats changed, nor was the smell of fire upon them. Then Nebuchadnezzar said, "Blessed be the God of Shadrach, Meshach, and Abednego who has sent His Angel (the Angel of the Lord, the Redeeming Angel, Christ Himself) and delivered His servants that trusted in Him. He has changed the king's word, and yielded their bodies that they might not serve or worship any god except their own God. Therefore, I make a decree that every people, every nation, every language which speak anything against the God of Shadrach, Meshach, and Abednego shall be cut into pieces, and their houses shall be made a dunghill because there is no other God that is able to deliver after this sort."

Then the king promoted Shadrach, Meshach, and Abednego in the province of Babylon. And Nebuchadnezzar the king said unto all the people, all the nations, all the languages that dwell in all the earth, "Peace be multiplied unto you. It has seemed good unto me to declare the signs and wonders that God most high has wrought toward me. How great are His signs! And how mighty are His wonders! His kingdom is an ever-lasting kingdom, and His dominion is from generation to generation." The king had come to know the living God, Jesus Christ. He knew the Lord had touched him. Praise God.

Because Meshach, Shadrach, and Abednego trusted God, God was glorified, His name was lifted up.

The fourth conflict in the life of Daniel demonstrated that you cannot make an affirmation of faith, you cannot profess publicly that you acknowledge Christ as your living Lord and invite Him into your heart as your personal Savior and then turn around and take His praise, His honor, and His glory for yourself.

Now Nebuchadnezzar had another dream that made him afraid, and again he called in the Chaldeans and the astrologers and asked them to tell him the interpretation of his dream. Again, they were not able to do it. So he called for Daniel and told him the dream and asked him to interpret it. And Daniel told him the interpretation of the dream as God revealed it to him and exactly what was going to happen to him because he had become so arrogant and full of pride.

Then Daniel pleaded with the king, "O King, let my counsel be acceptable to you. Break off your sin, break off your sin of arrogance before God. Break off your sin by giving alms to the poor, by taking care of the widows, the orphans. Break off your iniquities, O King, by showing mercy to the poor, that there may be a lengthening of your prosperity. Perhaps if you do this, if you repent of that which you have been doing which is not right with the Lord, perhaps the Lord will permit Himself to be entreated by your prayer."

But King Nebuchadnezzar did not listen. A full year passed after the dream and its interpretation and Nebuchadnezzar had shown no repentance. He was walking upon the royal palace of Babylon, saying, "Is not this great Babylon which *I* have built for a royal dwelling place by the might of *my* power, and for the glory of *my* majesty?"

While the word was still in the king's mouth, there came a voice from heaven, saying, "O King Nebuchadnezzar, I sent you Daniel to speak to you, to give you warning, far in advance. But you refuse to heed, you refuse to be obedient, and the kingdom is departed from you. And you shall be driven from men, and your dwelling shall be with the beasts of the field. You shall have the heart of a beast, because you have acted as a beast. You shall be made to eat grass as oxen. And seven times—seven years—shall pass over you until you know, until you realize, that the most High rules in the kingdom of men, that Christ is king. He gives the kingdom to whomsoever He will."

That very same hour was the thing fulfilled upon Nebuchadnezzar. He was driven from men, and for seven years he did eat grass as oxen, and his body was wet with the dew of heaven, till his hair was grown like eagles' feathers, and his nails were like birds' claws.

Our rabbis say the Lord put him in this situation to

humble him, to bring him to the point of salvation, to cause him to die a saved man, knowing the Lord.

At the end of the seven years, Nebuchadnezzar was a changed man. He said, "I lifted up my eyes unto heaven, and my understanding returned to me, and I blessed the most High, and I praised and I honored Him. He lives forever, His dominion is an everlasting dominion, and His kingdom is from generation to generation. And all inhabitants of the earth are accounted as nothing. And He does according to His will in the host of heaven and among the inhabitants of the earth, and none can stay His hand, or say unto Him, 'What doest Thou?'"

And Nebuchadnezzar went on speaking, "At the same time, my understanding returned unto me, and for the glory of my kingdom, my majesty, my splendor returned unto me, and my ministers and my lords came out and sought me. I was established in my kingdom, and surpassing greatness was added unto me."

If he was great before, he was greater now that he gave the glory to God. "I, Nebuchadnezzar, praise, extol, honor the King of heaven, for all His works are truth, all His ways are justice, and those that walk in arrogance, He will abase." Being abased by God, Nebuchadnezzar was finally lifted up, when he came to repentance unto the Lord, and was obedient to praise Him and to give Him the glory.

The fifth conflict in the Book of Daniel involved the impious sacrilege arrayed against the reverence to the sacred objects of God, the vessels that had been brought in from the temple of the living God.

Belshazzar, the king, made a great feast to a thousand of his lords, and drank wine before the thousand. Belshazzar, while he tasted the wine, commanded to bring the gold and silver vessels which Nebuchadnezzar, his father, had taken out of the temple, which was in Jerusalem, that the king, and his lords, and his wives, and his concubines, might drink therefrom. They were going to desecrate and defile the holy objects of the Lord. The Lord had commanded that only the Levites could handle the sacred objects of the Lord. They were dedicated unto the Lord. No other person could touch them, not from any other tribe.

Then they brought in the golden vessels that were taken out of the temple of the house of God which was at Jerusalem; and the king, and his lords, and his wives, and his concubines, drank from them. They drank wine, and praised the gods of gold, and they praised the gods of silver. They praised the gods of brass. They praised the gods of iron. They praised the gods of wood. And they praised the gods of stone.

In the same hour, came forth fingers of a man's hand. It was the beautiful hand of Jesus writing on that wall. The fingers of the man's hand wrote over against the candlestick upon the plaster of the wall of the king's palace; and the king saw the part of the hand that wrote.

Then the king's countenance was changed, and his thoughts troubled him, the joints of his loins were loosed, and his knees smote one against another. He was trembling and shaking. All of his joints were falling apart.

The king cried aloud to bring in the magicians, the sorcerers, those who were tied up with witchcraft, the enchanters, the Chaldeans, the soothsayers. And the king spoke and said to those wise men of Babylon, "Whosoever shall read this writing, and show me the interpretation thereof, shall be clothed with purple, have a chain of gold about his neck, and he shall be the third ruler in the kingdom."

Then came in all the king's wise men, but they could not read the writing, nor could they make known to the king the interpretation. Then was King Belshazzar greatly troubled, his countenance was changed in him, and his lords were perplexed.

Now the queen by reason of the words of the king and his lords came into the banquet house. The queen spoke and said, "O King, live forever: let not your thoughts trouble you, nor let your face be changed. Don't let your face fall. There is a man in your kingdom in whom is the spirit of the holy gods; and in the days of your father, Nebuchadnezzar, light and understanding and the wisdom of God were found in him."

What did they see in Daniel? They had seen the Spirit of the living God, the Holy Spirit, in Daniel and upon him. And the queen remembered.

She went on to say, "And the king Nebuchadnezzar, your father, the king, made him master of the magicians, the enchanters, the Chaldeans, and the soothsayers. Forasmuch as an excellent spirit, and knowledge, and understanding, and interpreting of dreams, and showing of dark sentences, and dissolving of doubts were found in the same Daniel whom the king named Belteshazzar. Now let Daniel be called, and he will show you the interpretation."

Then was Daniel brought in before the king. And the king spoke and said unto Daniel, "Are you that very same Daniel who are of the children of the captivity of Judah, whom the king, my father, brought out of Judah? I have heard of you that the spirit of the gods is in you and that light and understanding and excellent wisdom are found in you.

"And now the wise men, the magicians, the enchanters have been brought in before me, that they should read this writing, and make known unto me the interpretation thereof: but they could not show the interpretation of the thing. But I have heard of you, that you can give interpretations, you can dissolve doubts. If you can read the writing, and make known to me the interpretation thereof, you shall be clothed with purple. You will have a chain of gold about your neck, and you shall be third ruler in the kingdom." (The first ruler in the kingdom was Nebuchadnezzar, who was still alive. The son was ruling, because Nebuchadnezzar was out eating grass. Daniel would be the third ruler.)

Then Daniel answered and said before the king, "Let your gifts be to yourself. Keep your gifts, and give your rewards to somebody else. Nevertheless, I will read the writing unto the king, and I will make known to him the interpretation.

"O thou king, the most high God gave Nebuchadnezzar, your father, the kingdom, and greatness, and glory, and majesty. And because of the greatness that He gave him, all the peoples, all the nations, all languages trembled and feared before him: whom he would he slew, and whom he would he kept alive, and whom he would he raised up and whom he would he put down.

"But when his heart became arrogant, and he lifted himself up against the Lord, and his spirit was hardened so that he dealt arrogantly, he was deposed from his kingly throne, and they took his glory away from him. And he was driven from the sons of men; and his heart was made like the beasts, and his dwelling was with the wild asses, and he was fed with grass like oxen, his body was wet with the dew of heaven, until he knew that the most high God ruled in the kingdom of men, and that He sets up over it whomsoever He will.

"And you his son, Belshazzar, you have not humbled your heart. You're still arrogant, and if you don't humble yourself before the Lord, the Lord will humble you.

"You have not humbled your heart, though you knew all this, but you have done what your father has done. You have lifted up yourself against the Lord of heaven, and you have brought the vessels of His house before you, and you and your lords, your wives, your concubines, your prostitutes, have drunk wine from them, and you have praised the gods of silver, gold, brass, iron, wood, and stone which see not, hear not, know not. And the God in whose hand your very breath is, and whose are all your ways, you have not glorified. You have not given praise, honor, and glory to the living God, but you have praised everything else that man and that God have made. You have worshiped the creation instead of the Creator."

Then was the part of the hand sent from before him, and this writing was inscribed: MENE, MENE, TEKEL, UPHARSIN.

Daniel said, "This is the interpretation of the thing: MENE; God has numbered your kingdom, and He has already brought it to an end. You have been passed from grace into judgment. There's no salvation left for you, because you have lifted yourself up so high in arrogance against the Lord.

"TEKEL; You are weighed in the balance and you are found wanting.

"PERES; Your kingdom has been divided and given to the Medes and the Persians. They will come and take the kingdom away from you."

Then commanded Belshazzar, and they clothed Daniel with purple and put a chain of gold about his neck, and they made proclamation concerning him, that he should be the third ruler in the kingdom.

And in that night, Belshazzar, the Chaldean king, was slain.

The Lord had given the message, "Your kingdom has been brought to an end." That very same night, God kept His word. He will always do what He has promised—unless we, as a body of believers, intercede with Him.

He gave us the power of intercessory prayer. He says, "I will permit Myself to be entreated of you, but you have to humble yourself before Me. You have to be obedient and come to Me and ask Me, 'Lord, please change Your mind from that which You are about to do.'"

Judgment would not have come upon Israel if the people of Israel had been obedient unto the Lord. God spoke to Isaiah saying, "It amazes Me that there is not one intercessor found in all of Israel to intercede with Me and to petition Me for all of Israel."

The sixth conflict in the Book of Daniel was between malicious plotting and the providence of God over His saints. Darius the Mede became king of the Medo-Persian empire when he was about threescore and two years old. He had received the kingdom from God in fulfillment of the prophecy given by Daniel in the interpretation of the dream from Nebuchadnezzar. And it pleased King Darius, successor to Belshazzar, to set over the kingdom 120 satraps (princes) who would be throughout all the kingdom, and over them three presidents of whom Daniel was one, that these satraps might give account to them so that the king could suffer no loss or damage. Daniel was distinguished above the presidents and the satraps because an excellent spirit was in him, the Spirit of the Lord, the Holy Spirit, and the king sought to set him over the whole realm.

Then the presidents and the satraps sought to find some occasion to bring an accusation against Daniel concerning the kingdom, but they could find no occasion or any cause within him, for he was faithful, nor was there any error found in him whatsoever. Then said these men, "We shall not find any occasion to bring any accusation against this Daniel except we find it against him concerning the law of his God."

And so all the presidents of the kingdom, the deputies, the counselors, the governors, consulted and agreed that the king should establish a royal statute, make a firm decree that whoever should ask a petition of any God or man for thirty days except of the king should be cast into the den of lions. The decree, once passed, would be irrevocable. No one could change it.

King Darius signed the writing and the decree.

Now when Daniel knew that the writing was signed, he went into his house, and his windows being opened in his chamber toward Jerusalem, he faced toward Jerusalem, the way of the holy temple, got down on his knees three times a day, and prayed and gave thanks before his God as he had done previously. Nothing was going to change him, this circumstance, or any circumstance. He would remain obedient unto the Lord.

Then the men assembled, thronging, by agreement, and found Daniel praying and making supplication before his God. They came near and they said before the king concerning his prohibition and his decree, "O King, have you not signed an edict saying that any man that shall make a petition to any God or any man within thirty days, save you, O King, shall he not be cast into the den of lions?"

And the king answered and said, "The thing is true according to the law of the Medes and the Persians which cannot be changed or appealed."

And then they said before the king, "That Daniel, that no-good Daniel, who is one of the exiles from Judah, does not regard or pay any attention to you, O King, or to this decree that you have signed, but he makes his petition to his God three times a day."

Then the king, when he heard these words, was very much distressed over what he had done, that he permitted himself to sign this decree. And he set his mind on Daniel to deliver him, and he labored until the sun went down on how to rescue him.

Then these same men came thronging by agreement to the king and said, "Know, O King, that it is the law of the Medes and the Persians that no decree or statute which the king establishes may be changed or repealed." Then the king commanded, and Daniel was brought and cast into the den of lions.

And the king said to Daniel, "May your God whom you are serving continue to deliver you."

Praise God for the witness and the testimony of a man who will stand in spite of all circumstances and still remain obedient unto the Lord. Look at the witness. Many people may never read a Bible. The only Bible they will ever read will be you and me, and if we have professed with our lips that we are Christians, that we are Christlike, that we are a little Jesus Christ, they will read us. We will be their Bible. And if we are a false and poor witness for Jesus Christ, they're going to say, "If that's Christianity, I want no part of it."

Daniel was at the point where he had to stand on the promises of God. The Psalms are full of them!

"I sought the Lord, and He heard me, and delivered me from all of my fears.—The Angel of the Lord encampeth around about them that fear Him, who revere and worship Him with awe, and He delivereth them. —Many are the afflictions of the righteous; but the Lord delivereth him out of them all.—Mark the blameless man and behold the upright, for there is a happy end for the man of peace.—But the salvation of the consistently righteous is of the Lord. He is their refuge and secure stronghold in the time of trouble.—The Lord helps them and delivers them; He delivers them from the wicked and He saves them because they trust and take their refuge in Him—Call on Me, Jesus Christ, in the day of trouble, and I will deliver you. And you shall honor and praise Me and glorify Me.—I'm standing with you always."

Daniel in the lions' den called upon the name of the Lord.

A stone was brought, and laid upon the mouth of the den, and the king sealed it with his own signet and with the signet of his lords, that there might be no change of purpose concerning Daniel. And the king went to his palace and passed the night fasting. Neither were there instruments, nor music, nor dancing, nor girls brought before him as his sleep fled from him. He was interceding with the Lord for Daniels' life. He had seen the life of Christ coming through the life of Daniel.

As the king rose early in the morning, he went as fast as he could to the den of lions. And when he came to the den and to Daniel, he cried out in a voice of anguish, "O Daniel, servant of the living God, is your God whom you serve continually able to deliver you from the lions?"

Then Daniel said to the king, "O King, live forever. My God has sent His angel, His Redeeming Angel, my Jesus, and He has shut the lions' mouths, so that they have not hurt me, because I was found innocent and blameless before Him, before my God and also before you, my king. As you very well know, I have done no harm or wrong to anybody."

And the king was exceedingly glad, and he commanded that Daniel should be taken out of the den. So Daniel was taken up out of the den, and no hurt of any kind was found upon him because he believed, because he relied on, because he adhered to, because he trusted in his God, his Jesus Christ.

And king commanded, and those men who had accused Daniel were brought and cast into the den of lions, they, and their children, and their wives, and before they ever reached the bottom of the den, the lions had overpowered them, and had broken their bones in pieces.

Then King Darius wrote to all peoples, to all nations, to all languages in his kingdom and his empire that dwell in all the earth, saying, "Peace be multiplied unto you. I make a decree that in all my royal dominion, men tremble in fear before the God of Daniel, for He is the living God, He is enduring, He is steadfast, and He is the living God forever. His kingdom shall not be destroyed, and His dominion shall be even to the end of the world.

"He is a Savior, and He is a deliverer, and He works signs and wonders in the heavens and the earth, who has delivered Daniel from the power of the lions."

So Daniel prospered in the reign of Darius and in the reign of Cyrus the Persian. He was obedient unto the Lord. In every circumstance, he experienced the truth of God's promises. He knew God's divine protection: "I will not leave you; I will not forsake you; I will not fail you."

If we have to go into a fiery furnace, if we have to go into a lions' den, Jesus will be there.

Attempts to fit the prophecies of Daniel and Revelation into the facts and events of human history have produced an endless conflict of opinions.

Jesus said no man knows the time, the place, or the hour. When He was asked by His followers when He was coming back, He said, "Shortly." So they said, "Give us a sign, that we will know." He said, "No sign shall be given." "Right now, you are not going to

184

understand, but you will understand when I do ascend, and I will send you the Holy Spirit. Then He will reveal all things unto you. Everything will come back to your remembrance.

Do you notice the phenomenon of your obedience today when the Lord provides by divine appointment somebody for you to witness to? Scripture that you never even thought you knew is brought to your mind, and you quote one Scripture after another that you heard maybe five years ago, last month, last year. The Lord gives you the right Scripture, the right words, at the right time and the right place for you to plant the seed.

And He said, "Don't worry about that seed. I'll send somebody along to water it—and to harvest it. You just be obedient unto Me. I'll do the rest. Don't you play My part. Let Me be the Lord." He said, "My words will never come back void or empty. If you plant the word, I will make sure that it grows."

Two facts are generally acknowledged by most scholars concerning the prophecies and visions in Daniel and Revelation. One, that the prophecies represent a partially veiled revelation of future events in secular and sacred history. Two, that the visions point to the ultimate triumph of God's kingdom over all Satanic and world powers. Christ has defeated Satan and the world powers. He will be the King. There will be no other.

Many commentators see the four beasts in chapter 7 as representing the four great empires—Babylon, Persia, Greece, and Rome—followed by a vision of the coming Messiah, the coming Jesus.

In chapter 8, another period of the Medo-Persian-Grecian history appears under the figure of a beast.

Chapter 9 contains Daniel's prayer and a veiled prophecy of the time of the coming Messiah.

Chapters 10-12 contain additional far-reaching predictions and revelations of future events. These three chapters have been the battleground of theological controversy with many varied interpretations. Our own rabbis have taken the twelfth chapter of Daniel, and they have put the two numbers together with an interesting result.

Beginning with verse 8: And I heard, but I understood not: then said I, "O my Lord, what shall be the issue of these things?"

And He said, "Go your way, Daniel, for the words are shut up and sealed till the time of the end. Many people shall purify themselves and make themselves white and be refined, but the wicked shall do wickedly; none of the wicked shall understand, but they that are wise in the Lord, those who have the gifts of knowledge and wisdom from the Holy Spirit, shall understand. And from the time that the continual burnt offering shall be taken away, and the abomination that maketh desolate set up, there shall be a thousand two hundred and ninety days." The rabbis have interpreted this as twelve hundred and ninety years.

At the twelfth verse, we read, "Blessed is he that waits and comes to the thousand three hundred and thirty-five days." The rabbis have added the two figures together. Then, since the first destruction of the kingdom of Israel was in 721 B.C., they have subtracted 721 from 2625. The rabbis said that something miraculous would take place in 1904. And it did. That was the year of the Welsh revival, the great outpouring of the Holy Spirit, which spread and spread until it reached America in 1906. To this, the rabbis added seventy years—the temple was destroyed in 70 A.D. during the time of Titus. Seventy plus 1904—our rabbis have stated that the Messiah is coming in 1974. Based on the figures in the last chapter of Daniel, they're looking anxiously, awaiting Him.

There was an outpouring of God's Holy Spirit in the sixties, just as there was in the early period of our century. God is moving by His Holy Spirit in the seventies. We have not yet begun to see the miracles of the Holy Spirit. We've barely tasted a small portion, but we're going to see many, many things take place in the end times.

By our obedience, the Lord is preparing us as His Body of believers, His bride. We will all be sons and heirs with Him as we are obedient.

Praise the Lord!

Appendix
A Modern-Day Fleece

Is it wrong for Christians to set a fleece before the Lord? No. I don't see anything wrong with it at all, but a fleece has to be in the realm of the miraculous, something that cannot happen except by the divine intervention of the Lord.

Let me give you a modern-day example. While Steve, a good friend of mine, was ministering with us at Melodyland he got mixed up with a group of people whose preaching was not purely Scriptural. Though they urged the perfectly biblical example of selling one's goods and living in community (Acts 2:44-47), they preached in a spirit of exclusiveness. I could see it from where I stood, but Steve was so impressed with their moral earnestness and zeal that it completely escaped his notice.

I entreated him to remember that Jesus had said, "Be witnesses for Me in all the ends of the world. Make disciples of men everywhere, and preach the Gospel for Me." I wanted him to see that this group was preaching only a half-truth because of their exclusive spirit.

But Steve forgot what Jesus said, and became deeply involved in the wrong teaching.

"Well," he said, "if I'm on the wrong path, I'll have to have it proven to me."

"Would you be willing to set a fleece before the Lord?" I asked him.

He said yes. This was on Wednesday night.

"What's the hardest thing that you think the Lord can do for you?" I asked.

"Well," he said, "I have two missionary friends, a man and his wife. They're down in the jungle three hundred miles below Tijuana, Mexico, preaching the Gospel. I haven't heard from them in six years, and I'd like to know how they're getting along. But there's no way for me to get in touch with them."

I said, "How about if you ask the Lord to have them make the trip from where they are, cross the border at Tijuana, go into San Diego, pick up the telephone, and call you and say, 'Steve! How are you? How are you doing? What's going on?' We'll set the deadline at twelve o'clock noon on Friday." Steve liked the fleece, and conceded that it was in the realm of the miraculous, all right. If God honored that fleece, he'd admit that I was right about the false teaching.

And so we waited. Friday morning, I woke up at three o'clock looking at my watch. The Lord was really testing my faith. I sweated it out from three o'clock until twelve o'clock noon, and there was no phone call from Steve. It got to be five after twelve, ten minutes after twelve, and still no phone call.

At twelve fifteen, I couldn't stand it any longer. I called him. "Steve, what happened?" I asked him.

He said, "Praise the Lord! My friends called me at exactly twelve o'clock. They had made the journey across the border at Tijuana and picked up the phone in San Diego. They called up and said, 'Steve, how are you? How have you been? We haven't heard from you in such a long time. What's going on?'"

God had honored the fleece. Steve left that wrong group, came back to Melodyland, continued his studies, and today, he is in the ministry preaching the one true Gospel, being obedient to the Lord.

Any counseling requests, comments, inquiries for speaking engagements, or orders for tapes should be directed to Dr. Michael Esses, P. O. Box 3397, Orange, California 92665.